ORWELL IN AMERICA

For Joe —
for Christmas 2019.

Pam

Orwell in America

Thomas Fensch

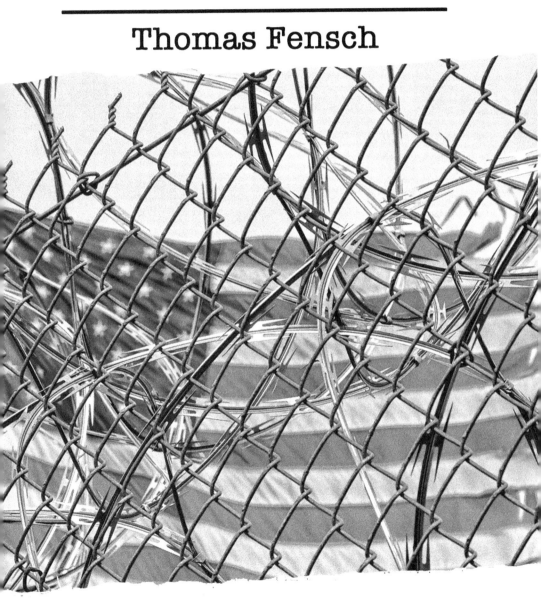

New Century Books

ISBN 978-1-7337852-0-4 Hardcover
ISBN 978-1-7326167-7-6 Paperback
ISBN 978-1-7337852-2-8 e-book

New Century Books
8821 Rockdale Rd.
N. Chesterfield, Va. 23236

newcentbks@gmail.com

Book design by Jill Ronsley, suneditwrite.com

for Rev. Fredrick Marcoux
with gratitude

Contents

1

Alexis De Tocqueville in America

Alexis De Tocqueville arrived in the United States in May, 1831, and departed its shore for his native France once again in February, 1832, only nine months later. Yet for considerably more than a century and half now, Tocqueville's *Democracy in America* has provided its readers an unparalleled abundance of description, analysis and prophecy concerning almost every aspect of the American scene.

… Richard H. Heffner writes in his Introduction to the 2010 edition of *Democracy in America*.

And, Heffner writes,

Born in Paris on July 29, 1805, Tocqueville was ascended from a proud old Norman family that for long generations had been considered among the *petite noblesse*. Thus it required no particular devotion to the villainies of the ancient regime to make Tocqueville initially suspicious of majority rule. The leveling doctrines of the French Revolution had already taken a heavy toll with his own family and circle of friends. During the revolution his parents had been jailed, his maternal grandfather, the Marquis of Rosambo, had been guillotined in the name of "Liberty, Equality and Fraternity." And though his Father was ultimately returned to rank and position after the fall of Napoleon, Tocqueville's own childhood had been overshadowed by memories of these earlier popular excesses. In so many ways, then, he was both by birth and by circumstances ideally suited to the role of hostile critic of democracy in America.

In essence, De Tocqueville was a classic liberal who advocated parliamentary government, but he was skeptical of the extremes of democracy.

In 1831, he obtained a mission (grant) from the French Monarchy to examine prisons and penitentiaries in the United States and journeyed to America from France with a lifelong friend, Gustave De Beaumont. Tocqueville did visit some prisons—but also traveled widely in the United States and took extensive notes about his observations and reflections.

Instead of writing about American prisons—he changed his focus and began a quite remarkable undertaking; nothing less than a comprehensive and detailed analysis of the state of the country as he saw it.

His analysis, *Democracy in America,* has been widely regarded since its first publication as one of the most influential books ever written about America.

He used the term the "tyranny of the majority," (as have others including John Stuart Mill) . He saw that public opinion could be a powerful force; that the majority could subjugate the minority and marginalize individuals; these ideas appear remarkably modern, but were first published in 1835, 184 years ago by now.

For those not familiar with *Democracy in America*, it is well worth listing the chapter headings:

PART ONE

PART TWO
BOOK 1

INFLUENCE OF DEMOCRACY UPON THE ACTION OF INTELLECT IN THE UNITED STATES

BOOK II

INFLUENCE OF DEMOCRACY ON
THE FEELINGS OF THE AMERICANS

Book III

INFLUENCE OF DEMOCRACY ON MANNERS PROPERTY SO CALLED

BOOK IV

INFLUENCE OF DEMOCRATIC IDEAS AND FEELINGS ON POLITICAL SOCIETY

52. Equality Naturally Gives Men a Taste for Free Institutions
53. That the Options of Democratic Nations About Government Are Naturally Favorable to the Concentration of Power
54. That the Sentiments of Democratic Nations Accord with Their Opinions in Leading Them to Concentrate Political Power
55. Of Certain Peculiar and Accidental Causes, Which Either Lead a People to Complete the Concentration of Government, or Which Divert Them from It
56. What Sort of Despotism Democratic Nations Have to Fear
57. General Survey of the Subject

De Tocqueville was more prescient that he could have imagined. In *Democracy in America* he forecast the prominence of the United States and Russia as the two main global powers. He wrote:

> There are now two great nations in the world, which starting from different points seem to be advancing toward the same goal: The Russians and the Anglo-Americans ... Each seems called by some secret design of Providence one day to hold in its hands the destinies of half the world.

Vartan Gregorian contributed a 13-page Afterward to the 2010 Signet paperback edition of *Democracy in America*. He writes:

In post-9/11 America, where we may all feel equally endangered the question of how much of our freedom—enshrined in our Constitution and the Bill of Rights—we are willing to sacrifice security is still an issue that remains open for discussion.

He cites Dostoevsky, media critic Marshall McLuhan, Rousseau, Bill Moyers, historian Garry Wills, and others—and he cites George Orwell. Extensively.

Gregorian writes:

But—to paraphrase Lincoln in the service of making an obvious point—all the people cannot govern all of the time. George Orwell's *1984* builds a nightmare world out of that notion, envisaging a society in which a faceless monolithic governing system has taken hold and purports to be the true representative will of the governed. Given those conditions, in the book, the only permissible political act in this society is abject adoration of the leader, Big Brother. Not only human life but human nature is controlled at all levels. There is no pity, love or family; it is a society in which children not only betray their parents, but parents are proud of such keenness and Party spirit in their malicious offspring.

But this is also a society that goes beyond such trappings of totalitarianism to achieve the ultimate in control and dehumanization: in the society of *1984*, all are deprived of both past and future, and each lives locked in a perpetual present. A Party slogan says, "Who controls the past controls the future; who controls the present controls the past." The past is constantly being fabricated, distorted, or destroyed. No documentation of it exists; all papers, books, notes, etc., are rewritten and the originals sent into the "memory hole." Even the literature and the language of the past are destroyed and replaced by gibberish versions in the language of Newspeak, which has as one of its goals the removal of any word constructions that might exemplify the ideas of freedom, liberty, rebellion, and so on. One character says admiringly of the shrinking volume of the new dictionary: "It's a beautiful thing, the destruction of words."

It is not just the written past that is manipulated. And destroyed, however. Human memory has become just as variable and erasable. Winston Smith, whose daily job in the Ministry of Truth is to rewrite and erase the past, commits the greatest crime in this society—he re-members the past and he pursues it. Winston seeks any fragment untouched by the Party that embodies the past—a glass paperweight, an old-fashioned room in a secondhand shop, an elderly man who can tell him how life really was like before the revolution that brought the Party to power. As he says "If the Party could thrust its hand into the past and say of this or that event, it *never happened,* that, surely was more terrifying than mere tor-ture or death."

The society of *1984* not only rejects history as the memory and record of human achievements, triumphs, follies and failures but, along with it, the notion that history teaches us of growth and progress and of the possibilities of an infinite advance for mankind. *1984* rejects our culture, values and humanistic traditions of Western and non-Western societies. It rejects the individual as a unique being, a unique moment in the universe, a rational, spiritual being, torn between the finite and the infinite, between morality and immortality, security and freedom, between agony and the pain of struggle and the joy and ecstasy of being and becoming.

…and a key question …

In any of his books, diary entries, essays, notes, plans or conversations with his wife, friends or colleagues, did Orwell ever think of journeying to America to write a De Tocqueville-type update? A *Nineteen Eighty-Four*-in-America project? A matching volume or American sequel to *Nineteen Eighty-Four*?

Hold that thought.

2

Eric Blair Becomes George Orwell

Like others before him, including Mark Twain—Eric Blair—born June 2, 1093 and died January 21, 1950—had world experiences fundamental to his writing.

He was born in India, to a family genteel but not wealthy. His father worked in the India Civil Service. A year after he was born, his mother took him and his two sisters to live in England, presumably for a better life. Blair saw his father briefly in 1907, when his father was on leave, but not again until 1912. Blair's school years were abysmal. He hated his first school, St. Cyrian's, in East Sussex. He described his next school, Wellington, as "beastly," but apparently was happier, when he reached Eton.

(His health problems, which would plague him throughout much of his life—eventually diagnosed as tuberculosis—may have begun, undiagnosed, during his time at Eton.)

Financially he couldn't afford further university work—moving from Eton to Cambridge University—without scholarship help, which didn't look promising; he thus decided to leave England. In October, 1922, he traveled through the Suez Canal and Ceylon and arrived in Rangoon in November to join the Indian Imperial Police. He was posted in the Irrawaddy Delta area, then closer to Rangoon.

He gained responsibility there quite young; while his contemporaries in England were still in school. He learned the Burmese language but contracted dengue fever in 1927. He took leave, returned to England, examined his life and resigned from the Indian Imperial Police to become a writer.

Like Mark Twain, and others before him, he mined his travel experiences; his novel *Burmese Days* (to be cited later) was published in 1934.

Down and Out in Paris and London—1933

In the spring of 1928 he moved to Paris where he lived in the Latin Quarter, where F. Scott Fitzgerald and Ernest Hemingway had also lived.

He fell seriously ill in March, 1929, and was taken to a charity hospital.

Subsequently an encounter with a "trollop," (his words) led to his first book.

He had taken this girl or woman to his quarters; she subsequently stole all his money; an incident, unfortunate at the time, which led to him taking jobs as the most menial of kitchen help in Paris restaurants—

Aside from the fact that he needed money immediately after the theft (the robber was described as an Italian male in the published book, not a trollop, so as not to offend his parents, still alive), why did he choose to work in the lowest-of-the-low dishwashing and kitchen help jobs in Paris, earning barely enough to stay alive day by day, week by week?

(Orwell uses the French word *plongeurs;* those who wash dishes and carry out other menial tasks in restaurants.)

It was a combination of work to stay alive and work to collect material for—well, for a book.

And why did he consider such a book about his lost days in Paris restaurant basements, in filth and heat, barely staying alive?

Four reasons, perhaps:

- The mad self-challenge of any writer and any *writing project: Can I do this? Will this work?*
- The chance to move as far away as possible, psychologically, from his Eton-British background;
- It may have been a *paean* to Jack London, a writer he highly respected or even revered;
- It may also have been his personal *atonement* for his years in Burma helping prop up British Colonialism.

He returned to England and discovered he didn't have quite enough material for a normal-length book and subsequently added material about being a poverty- stricken tramp in England, thus the eventual title.

His descriptions of the effects of poverty are instructive— and striking:

> It is altogether curious, your first contact with poverty. You have thought so much about poverty—it is the thing you have feared all your life, the thing you knew would happen to you sooner or later; and it is all so utterly and prosaically different. You thought it would be quite simple; it is extraordinarily complicated. You thought it would be terrible; it is merely squalid and boring. It is the peculiar *lowness* of poverty that you discover first; the shifts that it puts you to, the complicated meanness, the crust-wiping.

> You discover, for instance, the secrecy attaching to poverty. At a sudden stroke you have been reduced to an income of six francs a day. But of course you dare not

admit it—you have got to pretend that you are living quite as usual. From the start it tangles you in a nest of lies and even with the lies you can barely manage it.

* * *

You discover what it is like to be hungry. With bread and margarine in your belly, you go out and look into shop windows. Everywhere there is food insulting you in huge wasteful piles …

* * *

You discover the boredom which is inseparable from poverty; the times when you have nothing to do and, being underfed, can interest you in nothing.

* * *

This—one could describe it further, but it is is all in the same style—is life on six francs a day. Thousands of people in Paris live it—struggling artists and students, prostitutes when their luck is out, out-of-work people of all kinds. It is the suburbs, as it were, of poverty.

And, he writes …

Clothes are powerful things. Dressed in a tramp's clothes it is very difficult, at any rate, for the first day, not to feel that you are genuinely degraded. You might feel the same shame, irrational but very real, your first night in prison.

And finally …

And there is another feeling that is a great consolation in poverty. I believe everyone who has been hard up experienced it. It is a feeling of relief, almost of pleasure at knowing yourself at last genuinely down and out. You have talked so often of going to the dogs—and well, here are the dogs and you have reached them, and you can stand it. It takes off a lot of anxiety.

Orwell's first draft, without the down-and-out-in-London second part was sent to the British publishing firm Jonathan Cape, which rejected it. A year later, with the second part added, the manuscript was sent the firm of Faber and Faber, where T.S. Eliot was an editor. It was rejected there too. Finally, a chance encounter (as these things sometimes happen) gave the project a second life. A Blair family friend, Mabel Fierz and her husband, knew a literary agent, Leonard Moore. He sent the manuscript to a newly-established publishing firm, headed by Victor Gollancz; he wanted the manuscript. During the usual back-and-forth between author and editor *can we do this? should we do that?* Gollancz and then-Eric Blair had to decide on a title … and Blair's by-line.

Gollancz's first title suggestion was *Confessions of a Down and Out*: Blair was skeptical. Gollancz changed it at the last minute to the permanent title: *Down and Out in Paris and London.*

Then there was the question of Blair's by-line. He did not want the book published under his own name; he wanted to be a cipher, unknown, and thus able to investigate, and write about, societal-political issues which consumed him. Pseudonym suggestions were "X," "P.S. Burton," the name he used during his forays into the depths of poverty and "H. Lewis Allways." Finally he settled on Orwell, from the river Orwell in Suffolk. And George, surely a quintessentially British name.

Down and Out in Paris and London was first published in January, 1933; it was subsequently published in the United States by Harper & Brothers, Sales were slow until December 1940 when Penguin Books printed 55,000 paperback copies for sale in England.

(The idea of a paperback publishing began in England before World War Two and in the United States largely after World War Two.)

All Eric Blair's books were published under the George Orwell pseudonym.

And, with the subsequent publication of *Animal Farm,* first published in 1945 and *Nineteen Eighty-Four,*[1] first published in 1949, the pseudonym George Orwell became one of the four most universally-recognized pen names in the world.

Burmese Days—1934

George Orwell's first novel, *Burmese Days,* was a direct result of his five years' service—1922-1927—in the Indian Imperial Police in Burma (now Myanmar). At the time Burma was part of British Colonialism; it was governed by Great Britain from India—Orwell saw it all ebbing away and was outraged by what he saw.

Burmese Days describes "corruption and imperial bigotry" in a society where "after all, natives were natives—interesting, no doubt, but finally an inferior people." Those devastating comments were on the outside back cover of an early paperback edition of the novel.

Critics have noted Orwell's debt to Joseph Conrad, Somerset Maugham and most particularly, for *Burmese Days,* to E.M. Foster:

Jeffrey Meyers, in a 1975 guide to Orwell's work ... wrote that ...

> *Burmese Days* was strongly influenced by *A Passage to India,* which was published in 1924 when Orwell was

---

1 Note; subsequent editions—and critical studies of *Nineteen Eighty-Four* have shorted the title to *1984,* which we are using here.

serving in Burma. Both novels concern an Englishman's friendship with an Indian doctor, and a girl who goes out to the colonies, gets engaged and then breaks it off. Both use the Club scenes to reveal a cross section of colonial society, and both measure the personality and value of the characters by their racial attitudes ... But *Burmese Days* is a far more pessimistic book than *A Passage to India,* because official failures are not redeemed by successful personal relations.

And, Orwell later wrote, in *Why I Write* (1946):

I wanted to write enormous naturalistic novels with unhappy endings, full of detailed descriptions and arresting similes, and also full of purple passages in which my words were used partly for the sake of their sound. And in fact my first complete novel, *Burmese Days* ... is rather that kind of book.

His protagonist, James Flory, has been described as "the lone and lacking individual trapped within a bigger system that is undermining the better side of human nature."

As an Orwell friend, T.R. Fyvel, has written:

"From Flory in his first novel *Burmese Days* to Winston Smith in *1984,* his last, all his heroes are Orwell himself, suitably transmuted."

Orwell portrays him as:

Flory was a man about thirty-five, of middle height, not ill made. He had very black, stiff hair growing low on his head, and a cropped black mustache, and his skin, naturally sallow, was discolored by the sun. Not having grown fat or bald he did not look older than his age, but his face was very harried in spite of the sunburn, with lank cheeks and a sunken, withered look round the eyes.

He had obviously not shaved this morning. He was dressed in the usual white shirt, khaki drill shorts and stockings, but instead of a topi he wore a battered Terai hat, cocked over one eye. He carried a bamboo stick with a wrist-thong, and a black cocker spaniel named Flo was ambling after him.

All these were secondary expressions, however. The first thing that one noticed in Flory was a hideous birthmark stretching in a ragged crescent down his left cheek, from the eye to the corner of the mouth. Seen from the left side his face has a battered, woe-begone look, as though the birthmark, had been a bruise—for it was a dark blue in color. He was quite aware of his hideousness. And at all times, when he was not alone, there was a sidelongness about his movements, as he maneuvered constantly to keep the birthmark out of sight.

Flory's birthmark, or facial scar, which he turns away from those in front of him, is a stark foreshadowing of the denouement of the novel.

Topics in *Burmese Days* include: British Colonialism, which Orwell saw ebbing, or perhaps rotting, away; and identity of those in Burma—the British officials tasked with preserving the British empire while in service there, trapped between British rule and the native Burmese culture. One of the characters calls the native Burmese people "black stinking swine."

Identity leads to the denouement of the book. Because of possible libel problems in England, *Burmese Days* was published first in the United States. Harpers published the novel in October, 1934, with a printing of 2,000 copies. In February, 1935, only four month later, 976 copies were remaindered, or sold off for pennies on the dollar. (The first British edition of *Homage to Catalonia* met the same fate, to be cited later.)

At the same time, in England, Orwell had to wrestle with his publisher Victor Gollancz, to publish the book. Gollancz first rejected it, based on legal problems he was having with another book and another author—not Orwell—although he had published *Down and Out in Paris and London.*

The British publishers Heinemann and Jonathan Cape also rejected it. Finally Gollancz agreed to publish it after Orwell made assurances that names and situations could be changed so there would be no libel issues. The book was finally published by Gollancz in England June 24, 1935.

Some British hands still in Burma believed that Orwell "rather let down our side." Or, they implied, he was, as was oft-said of Franklin Roosevelt, a "traitor to his class."

In 1946, Orwell wrote "I dare say it's unfair in some ways and inaccurate in some details, but much of it is simply reporting what I have seen." Orwell's reportage would come into exact focus in *Homage to Catalonia,* later.

In 2013, The Burmese Ministry of Information named the new translation (by Maung Myint Kywe) of *Burmese Days,* the winner of the 2012 Burma National Literature Award's "informative literature" (translation) category. The National Literary Awards are the highest literary awards in Burma.

A Clergyman's Daughter—1935

After retiring from Paris in 1929 for the experiences which led to Down and Out in Paris (finally published as *Down and Out in Paris and London)* Orwell lived in the home of his parents on the Suffolk coast. He subsequently spent two months, August and September, 1931, picking hops in Kent, lived like other hop pickers and kept a journal. Much of the journal appeared in *A Clergyman's Daughter.*

He began writing *A Clergyman's Daughter* in mid-January, 1934, and finished it early October, 1934. It was his most experimental book, owing some to James Joyce and *Ulysses*. Christopher Hitchens, in *Why Orwell Matters* states that Orwell apparently took the title from Ulysses:

> How now, sirrah, that pound he lent you when you were hungry?
> Marry, I wanted it.
> Take thou this noble.
> Go to! You spent most of it in Georgia
> Johnsons's bed, clergyman's daughter.

In this novel, the heroine—if she may be called that—is Dorothy Hare, who was the weak-willed daughter of a disagreeable widowed clergyman. This is the old American Horatio Alger self-made success books, but in bleak reversal.

She suffers amnesia, and loses track of eight days. She, like Orwell, worked in the hop fields for very little wages. She travels to London, but as a single woman with no luggage, is not allowed to stay at respectable hotels. She is forced to sleep in the streets, also much like Orwell in Paris.

Throughout the novel, she is a victim, psychologically dependent on others and without sufficient income to sustain herself. Orwell paints the same picture of deep, wrenching, lower-class poverty he revealed in *Down and Out in Paris and London*.

He critiques the school system in England, where there are "good boys," whose parents can pay full fees and the others—which included Orwell himself earlier, whose parents pay part of the tuition and Orwell, then, is treated as barely a second-class boy.

Orwell's publisher Victor Gollancz released it in March, 1935, after some minor revisions to avoid any possible libel suits.

Victor McHugh, reviewing the book in the *New York Herald Tribune,* compared the book to Dickens and George Gissing, whom Orwell admired:

> Mr. Orwell too, writes of a world crawling with poverty, a horrible dun flat terrain in which the abuses marked out by those earlier writers have been for the most part only deepened and consolidated. The stagers of Dorothy's plight—the coming to herself in the London street, the sense of being cut off from friends and the familiar, the destitution and the … nightmare in which one may be dropped out of respectable life, no matter how debt-ridden and forlorn, into the unthinkable pit of the beggar's hunger and the hopelessly declassed.

Orwell himself was never satisfied with the book. In a letter to one friend of he called it "tripe" and in another letter he said the book was even worse than *Keep the Aspidistra Flying* and "I oughtn't to have published it, but I was desperate for money."

He once stated that he didn't want the book to be reprinted after his death, but relented if it would "bring in a a few pounds for my heirs."

In truth, if it hadn't been for his later worldwide critical acclaim (and financial success) with *Animal Farm* and *1984, A Clergyman's Daughter* and *Keep the Aspidistra Flying* would have—and should have—completely disappeared decades ago.

Keep the Aspidistra Flying—1936

Orwell wrote this book in 1934 and in 1935 while living in a variety of apartments (flats) in the London area; he mined his previous experiences at being down and out and the dismal life he experienced living near- penniless .

(The Aspidistra in the title is a medium-size houseplant much prized during the Victorian era for its ability to withstand inadequate heat and inadequate indoor light, but which became a long-running national joke later; a bit of "hurray for the middle class" sarcasm.)

Orwell's protagonist, Gordon Comstock gives up his career with an advertising agency, "New Albion," to live a life of genteel poverty (much as Orwell's life had been, up to this point)—and writing poetry.

Comstock had "declared war" on money and a respectable life. But, as he discovered, neither the war on respectability nor the poetry went well. Under the stress of his self-imposed exile from affluence, he became absurd, petty and deeply neurotic. He is obsessed with what he calls "the Money God." He has a girlfriend, Rosemary Waterlow, whom he met at New Albion, but their relationship is marred by his self- imposed poverty. She works late; they have little time together. She lives in a hostel and his landlady forbids female visitors.

He sees money as the root of all evil and the root of everything that doesn't work in his self-imposed exile from middle-class respectability.

In the countryside, about to make love or have sex for the first time, she pushes him away—he wasn't going to use a prophylactic—a condom—which engendered this diatribe: "Money, again, you see! ... You say you, 'can't' have a baby ... you mean you daren't because you'd lose your job and I've got no money and all of us would starve."

Eventually he and she do have sex—she later tells him she's pregnant. Neither wants an abortion. He then is faced with a choice; leave her to remain in poverty—knowing the shame of her unwed pregnancy would bring to her family—or marry her and return to a respectable job at New Albion. He chooses New

Albion and returns to a middle class life. He throws away his poetry and returns to began work on an advertising campaign for a new product to prevent foot odor.

And ... he buys an aspidistra for their new middle-class flat.

The plot is predictable; the characters predictable and the denouement even more predictable. Orwell's female characters are better realized then in previous books, but even that isn't saying much (Orwell always had trouble with female characters up to and including *1984*) .

Orwell biographer Jeffrey Meyers found the book flawed by weaknesses in plot, style and characterization (what else is there?).

Orwell himself said it was "one of two, or three books, of which he was ashamed."

Reviews? *The New Statesman* referred to "clear and violent language, at times making the reader feel he is in a dentist's chair with the drill whirring."

And Norman Mailer said, "It is perfect from the first page to the last." *Really, Mr. Mailer, really?*

In order of excellence, from *1984* and *Animal Farm* through *Homage to Catalonia, Burmese Days, Down and Out in Paris and London* and *The Road to Wigan Pier, A Clergyman's Daughter* and *Keep the Aspidistra Flying* surely rank at the bottom of the Orwell canon.

The Road to Wigan Pier—1937

Orwell turned in his manuscript for *Keep the Aspidistra Flying* to his publisher Victor Gollancz January 15, 1936 and almost immediately Gollancz offered him a new project—Orwell would investigate the coal areas and associated poverty in northern England.

Gollancz was not only a publisher but a dedicated social reformer. In *Orwell: The Transformation*, Stansky and Abrahams write:

> As a social reformer, a socialist, and an idealist, Gollancz had an unquestioning, perhaps overly optimistic, faith in education; if only people could be made to know the nature of poverty, he thought, they would want to eradicate it, remove from power the government that tolerated it, and transform the economic system that brought it into being.

If Orwell didn't accept the project with avidity—he must have surely recognized that the project would be a mirror image of the Paris section of *Down and Out in Paris and London,* which in fact it was.

Orwell traveled to northern England—specifically the West Midlands area, Yorkshire and Lancashire—and stayed in the same wretched quarters he had lived in, during his down-and-out-in-Paris experience.

He chronicled housing in that region, mediocre at best; the plight of old-age pensioners, bereft of funds and security. He met local residents, talked, and observed the same type of squalor he saw in the lower depths of Paris (and London).

What he saw and learned:

He went down into the coal mines and discovered he was far too tall to be a miner; they were short, muscular and worked for hours and hours and hours on their knees. (Orwell had to crawl through some sections of some mines, on all fours.) And when they emerged from the mines, they were invariably covered with coal dust, which caused eventual eye problems and other occupational ailments. He discovered that many seemed to have odd blue, misshapen natural "tattoos" on their noses or foreheads—if they were cut or bruised, coal dust would seep into the cut or bruise and eventually turn an odd blue color. He learned that the braces for the mine tunnels were all wood; if stressed, the wood would creak and groan before breaking, thus giving the miners at last a momentary warning before a tunnel collapse. Metal braces would simply break without warning.

What he wrote:

In Chapter One, he describes the Brooker family, who had a bit more income than others in that locale, because they rented parts of their home to transients like Orwell, or more permanent guest-residents.

Chapter Two describes the life of coal miners, and includes Orwell's experiences in going down into coal mines. This is the most graphic part of the book.

Chapter Three discusses the average life of a coal miner: health and lack of financial security.

Chapter Four describes the housing situation in the West Midlands, Yorkshire and Lancaster areas— substandard housing with little incentive for anyone to offer anything better for the miners, who couldn't afford anything better anyway.

Chapter Five analyzes unemployment and employment statistics.

Chapter Six discusses food for the average miner—many suffered from malnutrition; Food for the miners and their families also sub-standard. Orwell lists the costs, in British currency, at that time, for the following, presumably a typical diet:

3 wholemeal leaves
1/2 lb. margarine
1/2 lb. dripping[2]

---

2 presumably a sauce or a gravy-type substance

1 lb. cheese

1 lb. onions

1 lb. carrots

lb. broken biscuits

lb dates

1 tin evaporated milk

10 oranges

Sub-standard diets for many were based on part on their …

- Inadequate wages from mining;
- Benefits from mining companies to workers which were also inadequate;
- Unemployment was rampant: Orwell called it "frightful." Government help for the unemployed also lacking.

Chapter Seven describes how slag-heaps made the landscape a nightmare.

He writes:

A slag-heap is at best a hideous thing, because it is so planless and functionless. It is something just dumped on the earth, like the emptying of a giant's dust-bin. On the outskirts of the mining towns there are frightful landscapes where your horizon is ringed completely round by jagged grey mountains, and underfoot is mud and ashes and overhead the steel cables where tubs of dirt travel slowly across miles of country. Often the slag- heaps are on fire, and at night you see the red rivulets of fire winding this way and that, and also the slow-moving blue flames of sulphur, which always seem the point of expiring and always spring out again.

Orwell saw nothing joyous, uplifting or positive in his journeys in northern England. Nothing at all.

* * *

Across the Atlantic and across the United States, at approximately the same time, another writer was researching and discovering exactly the same poverty, hopelessness and despair, and the similarities are remarkable ...

In the early 1960s, Philip Graham, then publisher of *The Washington Post,* described journalism as "the first rough draft of a history that will never be completed ..."

Graham's definition is now something of a classic definition of daily journalism, but it also applies to the journalistic background of John Steinbeck's *The Grapes of Wrath.*

First, Steinbeck's use of a non-fiction journalistic background is one of three key elements that contributed to the success of *The Grapes of Wrath.*

Early in his career, John Steinbeck attempted to be a reporter. In late 1925, to early 1926, he traveled from California to New York City and got a job as a laborer on the Madison Square Garden construction project. After he watched another worker fall to his death, Steinbeck quit, but with the help of an uncle, he remained in New York as a reporter on *The New York American.* As a newsman Steinbeck seemed to give a new meaning to the word *mediocre.*

As Steinbeck biographer Jackson Benson writes:

Years later he recalled that "they gave me stories to cover in Queens and Brooklyn and I would get lost and spend hours trying to find my way back." He also found himself getting emotionally involved with the people he was supposed to write about and then trying to kill the story to protect the people. With all his difficulties, his uncle's continuing influence with the editors apparently saved him, for instead of being fired, he was assigned to cover the federal courts in the old Park Row Post Office. But reporting the counts was a job for an experienced hand, not a cub. It required a knowledge of the system, the cultivation of inside sources and a nose for the telltale detail that covered a possible scandal. "They pretended that I knew what I was doing, and they did their best to teach me in a roundabout way. "

But Steinbeck was fired, He simply was not good enough. He took a slow boat back to California, "his tail between his legs."

How then did he do so well almost 10 years later, reporting on the migrants in California, in a series in *The San Francisco News,* titled "The Harvest Gypsies"?

Here are several answers. Steinbeck was out of his element in New York. He had just come from California at a time when idyllic California really was idyllic. He had no prior experience in journalism, and as much as he had studied at Stanford University (he left before graduating), there is no evidence that he ever paid much attention to journalism. He was lost in the biggest city in the country.

Like many other young people on their own in a big city, Steinbeck would take a job—any reasonable job—to make enough money for an apartment and steady meals. But New York City was—and still is—the most competitive city in the United States for journalism—and, at that time, Steinbeck simply was not a competitive journalist.

Jump now to the 1930s. The swirling wind storms that ruined many farms in the Midwest began with this decade.

Jackson Benson's summary of the migration of the Okies describes a result of these storms:

> Their exodus from the Dust Bowl started in 1930 and increased every year, So that by 1935-1936, 87,302 entered California that year. The total number of Dust

Bowl refugees that entered during the decade has been estimated at 300,000 to 400,000, an overwhelming number, considering that the total number of farm workers throughout the state prior to the influx was something over 200,000. They came with the vague idea that by heading west they might be able to get a new start, perhaps some land. But there was no land, and there was already a surplus of farm labor. At the end of Highway 66 in the Central Valley of California, they encountered an agricultural region that as probably the most industrially organized and most highly mechanized of any such area in the world.

There these fiercely independent small farmers found themselves looks down upon. Refugees from the Bible Belt whose strict fundamentalist Christianity was an important part of their culture … found themselves pilloried as having loose morals. A proud people who had scorned those who accepted "charity" found themselves starving for a lack of government relief. Texans who had no use for Mexicans found themselves competing with skilled Mexican field-workers for jobs, such as fruit picking and vegetable harvesting that they knew little about.

Californians with no ties to farming little realized the extent of the Okie invasion and much of the rest of the country knew nothing about what was happening in California. (At one point Steinbeck feared the state of California was close to civil war—between the growers and farm workers on one side and the migrants and Okies on the other.)

One newspaper that was aware of what was happening was *The San Francisco News*. *The News* was aware of the efforts of administrator Tom Collins to bring cleanliness to the migrant camps which he administered. One Steinbeck biographer writes:

The first camp was built near Maryville, north of Sacramento, in 19354, and one man named Tom Collins was chosen to run it. Collins was one of the people for whom adventure fiction is made, who turn up in a place, with a mysterious past, take hold of a difficult situation and handle it with nervy rigor and imagination then disappear. He not only ran labor camps, but evolved a philosophy and workable systems for them. After the Marysville camp was set up, another was built for Arvin, near Bakersfield, at the lower end of the San Joaguin Valley, and Collins moved there to run it.

One of his jobs was to keep weekly reports on doings at the camp, and he turned them into an odd literary form all his own—the most unlikely reports ever filed by a federal employee. They contained songs and poems and folk wisdom of the migrants, editorials on living conditions, journalistic accounts of life with hostile growers, and detailed inventories of the origins and possessions of the migrants.

Some of these reports were forwarded by Collins' superior to The *San Francisco News,* where they were excerpted; the *News* was a feisty Scripps-Howard newspaper, and about the only one to take a stand on the plight of the workers. It was only natural that when Steinbeck got his *News* assignment, one of the first people he looked up was Tom Collins.

Few people realize, however, that Steinbeck may have been approached previously with just about the same proposal. In a magazine article in the March, 1989, issue of *American Photographer* magazine, titled "Travels with Steinbeck," and sub-titled "Fifty years ago, *The Grapes of Wrath* shocked the world and brought fame to the author. But few know of the photographer behind the man who wrote the novel." David Roberts writes about Horace Bristol, a California photographer who had established a studio in San Francisco and who had met Ansel Adams, Edward Weston and Dorothea Lange. By the age of 28, Bristol had bene hired by *Life* magazine. Roberts writes:

> Guided by Lange, Bristol began to photograph the migrant farmers from Oklahoma who, driven from their homes by Dust Bowl drought, had flocked to California's Central Valley in a desperate search for work. He had been impressed and moved by a text-and-picture book about poverty in the south called *You Have Seen Their Faces*, a deft collaboration between photographer Margaret Bourke-White and novelist Erskine Caldwell.
>
> Bristol had a bright idea. Why not to do a kindred book about Okies in California? As he pondered what writer he might persuade to compose the text, an obvious name came to mind: John Steinbeck. Bristol has never met Steinbeck, but he had read *In Dubious Battle*, a novel that flaunted Steinbeck's sympathies with organized labor. Late in 1937, Bristol recalled, "I called Steinbeck on the phone and told him what I wanted to do. He said "Come on down and we'll talk about it." At the novelist's cottage in Los Gatos, Steinbeck and Bristol shared a leisurely lunch and two bottles of wine. Steinbeck thought Bristol was onto something important. He agreed too collaborate on the book.
>
> During five or six weekends in early 1938, the writer and the photographer drove to the Central Valley to gather material. They traveled widely, but both men were riveted by what they saw around the town of Visalia, where midwinter floods were taking a grim toll among Okies in starvation and disease.

"Steinbeck was wonderful," recalls Bristol. "The ease with which he worked with these people—they never felt defensive. They just opened up to him. He'd get talking to someone and I'd move in behind him with the camera."

Two or there months after their last trip to Visalia, Bristol called Steinbeck. "I said, 'I think I have enough pictures.' He said, 'Well, Horace, I have bad news for you. I'm going to write it as a novel.'"

This episode is not mentioned in Benson's *The True Adventures of John Steinbeck, Writer*, although Benson mentions that *Life* magazine published some of Bristol's migrant photos. Robert DeMott, at the end of the Introduction to *Working Days*, (Steinbeck's diary during the months he wrote *The Grapes of Wrath*) refers to the Bristol- Steinbeck anecdote and cites some additional Bristol publications, clarifying his work and his impressions of Steinbeck's work during those days.

But the Bristol episode illustrates several other important points.

If this Bristol episode has not been verified in all Steinbeck biographies, Steinbeck's work with Tom Collins is well known. Brian St. Pierre mentioned their collaboration in his book, *John Steinbeck: The California Years* as does Jackson Benson. St. Pierre writes:

> Most of Steinbeck's best work began with real people and first-hand observation, and in Tom Collins, he had the richest imaginable source and best guide. The *Grapes of Wrath*, which eventually came out of their friendship, is dedicated to him.

Jackson Benson relates this part of Steinbeck's life:

> In preparation for his trip and in order to travel among the migrants as unconsciously as possible, Steinbeck

bought an old bakery truck, a "pie wagon," as he called it, and outfitted it with blankets, food and cooking utensils. Then in late August he went to San Francisco to talk over his assignment with the editors at the *News* and get a briefing from federal officials at the Resettlement Administration regional headquarters. He talked to Fred Soule at the Information Division and was able to gather most of the general background and statistical data he needed for his articles.

The Resettlement Administration was having a hard time selling its program, and the possibly favorable publicity that might come from Steinbeck's series was given high priority. He then left for a tour of the San Joaquin Valley, accompanied by ex-preacher Eric H. Thomsen, who as Director in Charge of Management (for the migrant camp program) for Region IX.

Driving down through the Central Valley, the two were sought out and stopped at several squatters camps. Thomsen wanted to show Steinbeck the contrast between how the migrants lived on their own and how they lived at the sanitary camps provided by the government. Steinbeck had had some experience with hobo campus and labor campus, had seen the Hoovervilles[3] that dotted the countryside and the slum filth of those encampments appalled him. And the people—beaten-down, scorned, without hope and terrified of starvation—he couldn't get them out of his mind.

So Steinbeck completed his seven-part series "The Harvest Gypsies," which was published in *The San*

---

3 "Hoovervilles" were migrant or hobo camps, built from cardboard and other such flimsy materials and were named ironically after Herbert Hoover, who was President during the early years of the stock market crash and the Great Depression.

Francisco News Oct. 5-12, 1936. (And later, in *The Grapes of Wrath,* he used, as a key character an ex-preacher.

(Was the character of Jim Casey, based on Eric Thomsen?)

What can we learn from that series—and how can we judge Steinbeck's "new" attempt at journalism—after his failure a decade earlier in New York City?

"The Harvest Gypsies" is devoted (in order) to:

Section One: a General Introduction.

Section Two: The Squatters' Camps.

Section Three: The Small Farm Owner.

Section Four: The Federal Government.

Section Five: The History of One Family.

Section Six: Foreign Labor in California.

Section Seven: Suggestions for Humane Treatment of the Migrants and Prognosis for the Future.

In the First Section, Steinbeck begins with panoramic beginning or in journalistic terms a comprehensive *lede* (pronounced *leed):*

At this season of the year, when California's great crops are coming into harvest, the heavy grapes, the prunes, the apples and lettuce and the rapidly maturing cotton, our highways swarm with the migrant workers, that shifting group of nomadic, poverty-stricken harvesters drive by hunger and the the threat of hunger from crop to crop, from harvest to harvest, up and down the state and into Oregon to some extent, and into Washington a little. But it is California which has and needs the majority of these new gypsies. It is a short study of these wanderers that these articles will undertake. There are at last 50,000 homeless migrants wandering up and down the state, and that is an army large enough to make it important to every person in the state.

Despite one awkward sentence: "It is short study of these wanderers that these articles will undertake," Steinbeck provides not only an adequate, but an exceptional beginning to his series. One of the keys to the entire series of articles is observation: Steinbeck is, as always, a keen observer. And that is also a notable characteristic not only a reporter, but of a novelist as well. Steinbeck's series is filled with descriptive phrases, for example: "open rattletrap cars loaded with children and with dirty bedding, with fire-blackened cooking utensils."

Also, the articles are not inflamed. Steinbeck wants the reader to be touched by the circumstances, not his polemic. Two rules of reportage are that the reporter remains neutral and that the reporter does not add emotion through the addition of punctuation, such as an exclamation mark. In this series, Steinbeck's articles follow these rules.

We cannot know now how the editors at *The San Francisco News* might have edited Steinbeck's material: we have no first drafts of this series to compare with the final published versions. The newspaper does not exist today; thus we have no access to its records or file copies. Since the editors commissioned Steinbeck to write this series as a correspondent or free-lance writer, since they bought his by-line and since they left one awkward sentence in the beginning paragraph of the first article in the series, it is likely that they left Steinbeck's copy alone.

What journalistic shortcomings do we see in Steinbeck's "Harvest Gypsies" copy?

He includes few quotations. In the first article he quotes an anonymous boy: "When they need us they call us migrants and when we've picked their crop, we're bums and have to get out." At the end of the first article, Steinbeck offers a slightly longer quotation from a migrant mother who had just given birth to a still-born baby.

(Steinbeck used this same quotation in *The Grapes of Wrath.*)

He highlights no individuals. Throughout the series, Steinbeck offers vague portraits of individual migrants. (He probably realized that picturing one—or more—migrants might have distorted the series.)

'Steinbeck offers the reader composite pictures of several migrants or migrant situations he has observed.

In the first article Steinbeck introduces the plight of the migrants in California and the extent of the problem facing all Californians—natives and migrants.

In the second installment of the series, Steinbeck shows readers three levels of hopelessness inside the squatters' camps: the newly-arrived family, which still has some possessions, a little money and some hope for the future; the family that has lived in the camp a year or so, living in filth and squalor, with little money and little hope, and at the third level, the family that has no hope, no money and that has succumbed to illnesses and death.

Steinbeck writes:

> The next door neighbor family or man, wife and three children of from three to nine years of age, have built a house by driving willow branches into the ground and wattling[4] weeds, tin, old paper and strips of carpet against them. A few branches are placed over the top to keep out the noonday sun. It would not turn water at all.[5] There is no bed. Somewhere the family has found a big piece of old carpet. It is on the ground. To go to bed the members of the family lie on the ground and fold the carpet over them.

4 A misprint. He probably meant jamming.
5 i.e., is not a roof.

The three year old child has a gunny sack tied about his middle for clothing. He has the swollen belly caused by malnutrition.

He sits on the ground in the sun in front of the house, and the little black flies buzz in circles and land on his closed eyes and crawl up his nose until he weakly brushes them away.

They try to get to the mucous in the eye-corners. This child seems to have the reactions of a baby much younger. The first year he had a little milk, but has had none since.

He will die in a short time. The older children may survive. Four nights ago the mother has a baby in the tent, on the dirty carpet. It was born dead, which is just as well because she could not have fed it at her breast; her own diet would not produce milk.

After it was born and she had seen it was dead, the mother rolled over and lay still for two days. She is up today, tottering around.

The last baby, born less than year ago, lived a week. The woman's eyes have the glazed, faraway look of a sleepwalker's eyes. She does not wash clothes any more. The drive that makes for cleanliness has been drained out of her and she hasn't the energy. The husband was a sharecropper once, but he couldn't make it go. Now he has lost even the desire to talk. He will not look directly at you, for that requires will, and will needs strength. He is a bad field worker for the same reason. It takes him a long time to make up his mind, so he is always late in moving and late in arriving in the fields. His top wage, when he can find work now, which isn't often, is a dollar a day.

The children do not even go to the willow clump any more. They squat where they are and kick a little dirt. The father is vaguely aware that there is a culture of hookworm in the mud along the river bank. But he hasn't the will nor the energy to resist. Too many things have happened to him.

Jackson Benson writes: "The family Steinbeck was writing about was actually a composite of several families he had encountered in visiting one squatters' camp after another."

The use of composite characters is dangerous in journalism because the composite character may not be an accurate representation of one individual. In Steinbeck's day, such composite characters may have been tolerated in journalism—today such practices are unethical.

In the series' third part—the section devoted to the small farmer—we see a variety of journalistic elements in Steinbeck's prose. The opening sentence, "When in the course of the season the small farmer has need of an influx of migrant workers ..." sounds like Jefferson's "When in the course of human events ..." Again we see Steinbeck generalizing about the small farmer—no individual farmer is pictured. Rather Steinbeck summarizes all small farmers in California. He writes:

> It is rare for a small farmer to be able to plant and mature his crops without loans from banks and finance companies. And since these banks and finance companies are at once members of the powerful growers' associations, and at the same time the one source of crop loans, the force of their policies on the small farmer can readily be seen. To refuse to obey is to invite foreclosure or a future denial of the necessary crop loan.

In short, Steinbeck understood the interlocking nature of the banks and the large-scale farmers; how they could destroy the small farmer who didn't comply with the migrant-labor policies imposed by the farmers' association and banks.

Steinbeck was, for the series "The Harvest Gypsies," a true investigative reporter. He understood the politics and the policies of the stated and region: he could work well with experts like Tom Collins; he could talk easily with migrant families; he could write well; he was an excellent observer; and, he had the physical energy and stamina to conduct extensive research.

Moreover, he did not let his outrage cripple his aims or his prose. He told the story simply and effectively.

In the third article, we even see examples of the farmers's slang—Steinbeck talks about the "pusher," the field boss in the orchards and the "pacer," a rabbit-like picker, whose productivity all migrants attempted to match. Even though, Steinbeck admits, "it is often the case that the pacer's row is done over again afterwards."

In the fourth article, Steinbeck discusses the role of the federal government in the California migrant affair. Steinbeck observes that the cost to the federal government to erect the migrant camp in Arvin was $18,000. exclusive of the cost to rent the land. (It certainly shows the difference between Steinbeck's day and our own, when we realize that $18,000 may be the average cost of a modest used car.)

In the same article, Steinbeck discuses the democratic policies in the Arvin camp—including a dramatic section on "The Good Neighbors," the women's association. Steinbeck writes:

> (The association) takes part in quilting and sewing projects, sees that destitution does not exist, governs and watches the nursery, where children can be left while the mothers are working in the fields and in the packing sheds. And all of this is done with the outside aid of one manager and one part-time nurse. As experiments in

natural and democratic self-government, these camps are unique in the United States.

And, he writes:

When a new family enters one of these camps, it is usually dirty; tired and broken. A group from the Good Neighbors meets it, tells it the rules, helps it get settled, instructs it in the use of the sanitary facilities, and if there are insufficient blankets or shelters, furnishes them from its own stores.

Steinbeck even quotes the manager's logbook:

New arrivals. Low in foodstuffs. Most of the personal belongings were tied up in sacks and were in filthy condition. The Good Neighbors at once took the family in hand, and by 10 o'clock they were fed, washed, camped, settled and asleep.

In the fifth article, Steinbeck discusses one family—again probably a composite of several families. And he discusses this family, in terms of food and medical needs after their 15-year-old boy was arrested for stealing a metal piece of gear to sell for food. The father had sprained an ankle previously and re-injured it walking to town to free the son. The son subsequently died of a burst appendix suffered in the fields and left untreated. A young daughter became ill with influenza and the family did not have enough money for a doctor. "This can go on indefinitely," Steinbeck writes. "The case histories like it can be found in their (sic) thousands."

Steinbeck even cites the typical diets for migrant families:

Family of eight—Boiled cabbage, baked sweet
potatoes, creamed carrots, fried dough, jelly, tea.

Family of seven—beans, baking-powder, biscuits, jam, coffee.

Family of six—canned salmon, cornbread, raw onions.

Family of five—biscuits, fried potatoes, dandelion greens, pears.

These are dinners. It is to be noticed that even in these flush times there is no milk, no butter. The major part of this diet is starch. In slack times the diet becomes all starch, this being the cheapest way to fill up. Dinners during lay-offs are as follows:

Family of seven—beans, fried dough.

Family of six—fried cornmeal.

Family of five—oatmeal mush.

Family of eight (there were six children)—

Dandelion greens and boiled potatoes.

And again Steinbeck stresses childbirth:

The following is an example: Wife of family with three children. She is 38; her face is lined and thin and there is a hard glaze on her eyes. The three children who survive were born prior to 1929, when the family rented a farm in Utah. In 1930, this woman bore a child which lived four months and died of "colic."

In 1931 another child was born dead because a "han' truck fulla boxes run into me two days before the baby come." In 1932 there was a miscarriage. "I couldn't carry the baby because I was sick." She is ashamed of this. In 1933 her baby lived a week. "Just died. I don't know what of." In 1934 she had no pregnancy; she is also a little ashamed of this. In 1935 her baby lived a long time, nine months.

"Seemed for a long time like he was gonna live. Big strong fella it seemed like." She is pregnant again. "If we could get milk for 'um I'd guess it'd be better."

"This is an extreme case, but by no means an unusual one," Steinbeck writes. And we cannot but wonder if he had the Rose of Sharon end-of-Grapes *Of Wrath* sequence in mind at the time.

In the sixth article, Steinbeck discusses the waves of foreign labor which coursed through California: the Chinese; then the Japanese; the Mexican laborers. (By 1920 there were 80,000 foreign-born Mexicans in California, Steinbeck writes.) Finally Filipinos entered California in vast numbers. Again Steinbeck uses statistics clearly, although his phrase "little brown men" seems patronizing today: "Between 1920 and 1929, 31,000 of these little brown men were brought into the United States, and most of them remained in California, a new group of peon workers."

Finally, he warns discreetly that the Okies, the newest wave of labor in California, will not tolerate the same conditions which foreign labor tolerated: "Foreign labor is on the wane in California, and the future farm workers are to be white and American. The fact must be recognized and a rearrangement of the attitude toward and treatment of migrant labor must be achieved."

In the final article, Steinbeck suggests solutions for the problems of the Okies: since the Okies were former farmers, land should be leased from the state or from the federal government for their use; the state should erect simple homes for their use in areas where migrant labor is needed; crops use should be changed so migrant pickers are not needed so crucially; instruction in health techniques should be made available to migrant workers and migrant labor committees should be set up to govern migrant affairs.

The California Attorney General's Office should have the power to investigate cases of vigilante terrorism throughout the state. These and other suggestions—seem entirely logical to us in retrospect. In Steinbeck's day, they were considered as radical and dangerous notions.

How do do we judge Steinbeck's "Harvest Gypsies" series? He did everything well:

- The series was well-conceived and planned;
- Whether the proposed book with photographer Horace Bristol is an entirely accurate anecdote about Steinbeck, Bristol correctly observed "Steinbeck was wonderful. The ease with which he worked with those people—they never felt defensive. They just opened up to him";
- Steinbeck completely understood the underlying California politics—the interaction between the banks and the large farmer-growers;
- He worked with the right people get the information he needed, notably Tom Collins;
- He used statistics correctly in the series and even used the slang of the growers accurately;
- His anger at the injustices of the farming system in California was tempered by his style—the series is neither too sedate nor too polemical.

How do others view the "Harvest Gypsies"?

In *Working Days: The Journals of The Grapes of Wrath*, Robert DeMott says, "'The Harvest Gypsies' (were) hard-hitting, unflinching investigative reports … full of case studies, chilling factual statistics and an unsettling catalogue of human woes."

When they were first published, in 1936 (and again when they were printed in pamphlet form in 1938 as "Their Blood Is Strong"), Steinbeck's articles solidified his credibility—both in and out of the migrant camps—as a serious commentator. "The Harvest Gypsies" and (Tom Collins' continuing reports) provided Steinbeck with a basic repository of precise information and folk values.

"From his numerous field trips with Tom Collins, and from countless hours of listening to migrant people, working beside them, listening them and sharing their problems, Steinbeck drew all the correct details of human form, language and landscape that ensure artistic verisimilitude, as well as the subtler nuances of dialect, idiosyncratic tics, habits, and gestures, which animate fictional characterization," DeMott wrote in his Introduction to *Working Days.*

So the first key to the success of *The Grapes of Wrath* is: when Steinbeck needed to be, he became a gifted reporter. Earlier, in New York City, he did not "know the terrain, "and did not care as much about the people he met. But later, in California, he did care about the injustices of the migrant camps. He was not only an accurate observer, but he saw meaning in human events. He was outraged at what he saw, but channeled his outrage into exceptional nonfiction, then fiction.

And how did he use the material from "The Harvest Gypsies" in *The Grapes of Wrath?*

He knew he faced a problem with the novel.

He knew that when the novel appeared, critics could easily dismiss the book by saying "the Joads are fictional—that isn't the way it is in California at all."

So Steinbeck wove "The Harvest Gypsies" into *The Grapes of Wrath.* The articles constitute *intercalary* chapters (material inserted into a larger narrative). He discusses the used cars, the "jalopies," which the migrants used to drive to California: the "Good Neighbors" in the migrant camps and other factual material. How do they affect the novel? Simply stated, they serve as breaks in the narrative to give the reader some psychological distance from the characters and the plot.

Additionally, they serve to validate the novel. Using "The Harvest Gypsies" material as intercalary chapters proves the truthfulness of *The Grapes of Wrath.*

Later, when Daryl F. Zanuck was making the film version of The *Grapes of Wrath*—with a young Henry Fonda as Tom Joad— he wanted to know that the conditions were as Steinbeck said they were. So he sent detectives out to see how truthful Steinbeck had been. When they returned, their report was: "Conditions are worse than Steinbeck reported."

Not only was Steinbeck an excellent reporter when he needed to be, he used his facts to validate his fictional world.

* * *

Publisher Victor Gollancz commissioned Orwell to investigate and write about the poverty and hopelessness—notably the coal miners—in northern England.

The San Francisco News commissioned John Steinbeck to investigate and write about the poverty and hopelessness of the migrants—notably the Okies—in California.

Both were driven by the stark urgency of the truth. And both were morally offended by the hunger, unemployment and sheer despair of those they saw in front of them.

Would Orwell have known of Steinbeck's "Harvest Gypsies" series? No. Not a chance. When the articles were first published in *The San Francisco News,* they reached only the general San Francisco circulation area of the paper; there was no national distribution as only a few papers—*The New York Times* and *USA Today*—have today; nor were they apparently sent nationality through the wire services—the Associated Press or United Press, at the time.

In 1938, Steinbeck allowed the series to be reprinted as a pamphlet, by a concerned California civic group, the Simon J. Lubin Society. The articles were retitled "Their Blood is Strong." The pamphlet would not have reached England. *The Harvest Gypsies* was published in book form for the first time, in 1988 and reprinted in 2002.

Would Steinbeck have known about, or read, *The Road to Wigan Pier*? There is no record in the vast Steinbeck record, biographies or other material, that he had read, knew about, or mentioned Orwell, then or later.

(And neither Orwell or others in England, nor Steinbeck or any others in California, Washington, D.C., or elsewhere, could anticipate, or predict, the end of the Depression, not in England nor in California. In fact, the Depression in the United States began to end the day Japan attacked Pearl Harbor, December 7, 1941. The United States' entry into World War Two meant that all able-bodied men and women[5] joined the armed services and others went to work in factories, arming American for the fight. The Okies and others went to work in vast numbers in west coast armament and aircraft factories, where they eventually blended into the war effort.)

Steinbeck drove his pie wagon, full of blankets and supplies, to aid the migrants; Orwell clambered—and crawled—through coal mines to discover first-hand what mining was like.

The first seven chapters in *The Road to Wigan Pier* are Orwell's observations and reportage from the West Midlands, Yorkshire and Lancashire areas. The second part of the book,

---

5 The author's step-mother joined the Navy as a young woman and served two years as a code clerk in Washington, D.C., during World War Two. When she died at 100, in Ohio, in August, 2018, there was a full military honor guard at her gravesite.

beginning with chapter eight—from chapter eight through chapter 13—are essays about Orwell's beliefs about socialism, and why people should support it.

Gollancz, as a publisher, has based his publishing house on pacifist and socialist non-fiction. He had established the Left Book Club, the first book club in the United Kingdom. He desperately wanted Orwell's book—but only the observational—reportage first half. He asked Orwell (and then, perhaps, his literary agent, or perhaps the agent first, then Orwell), to delete the second half. Both refused. Orwell left for the Spanish Civil War. Gollancz then wrote an Introduction, distancing himself, his publishing firm and the Left Book Club from the book. His Introduction, one Gollancz biographer, Ruth Dudley Edwards, wrote was "full of good criticism, unfair criticism and half-truths."

Orwell's reportage from northern England resulted in him being placed under surveillance by the British government from 1936 to 1948—one year before the publication of *1984*.

Homage to Catalonia—1938

Orwell married Eileen O'Shaughnessy June 9, 1936.

Soon thereafter the crises began that would lead to the Spanish Civil War. Orwell followed these developments avidly. He decided to go to Spain and fight on the Republican side, against Franco and Hitler's legions, sent as a prelude or rehearsal for a later war.

The Spanish Civil War, 1936-1939, provided George Orwell the perfect opportunity to achieve his *true metier;* his reportage, observations *and* social- political criticism.

As biographer Peter Lewis writes:

> When the Fascist forces, led by General Franco, rebelled against the Republican government of Spain on July 18, 1936, people of Left-wing sympathies everywhere

felt passionately committed to the Republican cause. At that time the involvement of the Communists in the Spanish government and the arms it was soon getting from Stalinist Russia only confirmed to many the rightness of the cause. At last, it seemed to Orwell, democracy was standing up to Fascism. Two thousand volunteers from Britain went out to fight Franco in the International Brigade, in the spirit of crusaders for a new world, a dream of socialist brotherhood come true. They were as mixture of workers and intelligentsia, doctrinaire Communists and poets. Poets like Auden and Spender volunteered for service of a propagandist kind, others like Julian Bell and John Cornford died in the fighting. Among the exalted waves of idealists, as soon as he had delivered the manuscript of *Wigan Pier* in December, Orwell went.

Orwell truly had discovered his *metier*; he only then had to match subject and the self-examination he had experienced. He said:

> Every line of serious work I have written since 1936 has been written *against* totalitarianism and *for* democratic socialism as I understand it … Looking back I see that invariably where I lacked a political purpose that I write lifeless books and was betrayed into purple passages, decorative adjectives and humbug generally.

Orwell reached Spain Dec. 26, 1936. He found almost impossible situations there; the Republican side was rife with factions including Marxist groups and the United Socialist party, which distrusted each other.

He had first thought to be a war correspondent, but soon decided to join one of the militia units, then fighting Franco. He decided not to join the International Brigade nor Communist nor the Anarchist militias, but a small dissident Marxist group, the P.O.U.M.; the *Partido Obrero de Unification Marxists* or Workers' Party for Marxist Unity.

Eventually it was not a wise choice.

> "Orwell did not know that two months before he arrived in Spain, the (Soviet law enforcement agency) NKVD's resident in Spain, Alexander Orlov, had assured NKVD Headquarters, 'the Trotskyist organization POUM can easily be liquidated'—by those, the Communists whom Orwell took to be allies in the fight against Franco."

He was given two weeks' training and served with the P.O.U.M, from December, 1936 until June, 1937. That month, the P.O.U.M. was declared an illegal organization and the top officers arrested and imprisoned. Orwell was forced to hide for several days until he—and his wife—were able to flee Spain.

Orwell saw real action—in fact, he served with the P.O.U.M in the Aragon region for 115 days. He was granted leave and saw his wife Eileen in Barcelona. Returning to the front, Orwell was shot by a sniper May 20, 1937; hit in the neck, he was very nearly killed. He service in Spain effectively over, he was transferred from an aid station, then transferred to hospitals again and again, finally reaching Barcelona. On June 23, escaping from anti-P. 0. U. M. forces, he and his wife boarded a train from Barcelona to Paris. It was barely in time; on July 13, a deposition was presented to the Tribunal for Espionage and High Treason, Valencia, charging both Orwell and his wife with "rabid Trotskyism" and being agents for the P.O.U.M.

Barcelona fell to Franco's forces January 26, 1939.

Orwell begins *Homage to Catalonia* with this remarkable portrait of a soldier he had just met—he pictures him much like an artist with a sketch pad might have done:

In the Lenin Barracks in Barcelona, the day before I joined the militia, I saw an Italian militiaman standing in front of the officers' table.

He was a tough-looking youth of twenty-five or six, with reddish-yellow hair and powerful shoulders. His peaked leather cap was pulled fiercely over one eye. He was standing in profile to me, his chin on his breast, gazing with a puzzled frown at a map which one of the officers had open on the table. Something in his face deeply moved me. It was the face a man who would commit murder and throw away his life for a friend—the kind of face you would expect in an Anarchist, though as likely as not he was a Communist. There were both candor and ferocity in it; also the pathetic reverence that illiterate people have for their supposed superiors. Obviously he could not make head or tail of the map; obviously he regarded map-reading as a stupendous intellectual feat. I hardly know why, but I have seldom seen anyone—any man, I mean—to whom I have taken such an immediate liking. While they were talking round the table some remark brought it out that I was a foreigner. The Italian raised his head and said quickly:

"Italiano?"

I answered in my bad Spanish: "No, Ingles. Y tu?"

"Italiano."

He describes how the Communist hammer and sickle appeared as graffiti on nearly every wall in Barcelona and how the P.O.U.M. recruits seem to be boys of sixteen to eighteen who lacked adequate weapons, who seemed to have no conception of war. And how everything seemed to be put off off until *mañana* (tomorrow).

In subsequent chapters Orwell describes how he was supplied with …

> … a German Mauser (rifle) dated 1986—more than forty years old! It was rusty, the bolt was stiff, the wooden barrel-guard was split; one glance down the muzzle showed it was corroded and past praying for.

He was shot at for the first time near Zaragoza.

He describes the alphabet soup of names of trade unions and militia—which confused him:

> P.S.U.C., P.O.U.M., F.A.I., C.N.T., U.G.T., J.C.I., J.S.U., A.I.T.—they merely exasperated me. It looked at first sight as though Spain were suffering from a plague of initials.

On the east side of Huesca—he experienced nothing but boredom—and lice. One hand got inflected and he had to spend ten days in a "so-called" hospital in Monflorite, where attendants stole everything he had.

And rats. *Rats!* that were "really as big as cats, or nearly." Orwell apparently had a phobia for rats (and who wouldn't, at that size?).

Orwell's rat phobia (and his memory of one obscure book which he had read—to be cited later) clearly foreshadows one of the most horrific episodes in modern literature—Winston Smith's torture with hungry rats, toward the end of *1984*.

And, perhaps the most gripping episode in the book is Orwell's description of being shot by a sniper. He was near Huesca, where a bullet hit his neck and very nearly killed him. A fraction of an inch difference and he would have bled to death on the spot:

> It was at the corner of the parapet, at five- o'clock in the morning. This was always a dangerous time, because

we had the dawn at our backs, and if you stuck your head above the parapet it was clearly outlined against the sky. I was talking to the sentries preparatory to changing the guard. Suddenly, in the very middle of saying something, I felt—it is very hard to describe what I felt, though I remember it with the utmost vividness.

Roughly speaking it was the sensation of being *at the centre* of an explosion. There seemed to be a loud bang and a blinding flash of light all around me, and I felt a tremendous shock—no pain, only a violent shock, such as you get from an electric terminal; with it a sense of utter weakness, a feeling of being stricken and shriveled up to nothing. The sand-bags in front of me receded into immense distance. I fancy you would feel much the same if you were struck by lightning. I knew immediately that I was shot, but because of the seeming bang and flash I thought it was a rifle nearby that had gone off accidentally and shot me. All this happened in a space of time much less than second. The next moment my knees crumpled up and I was falling, my head hitting the ground with a violent bang which, to my relief, did not hurt. I had a numb, dazed feeling. A consciousness of being very badly hurt, but no pain in the ordinary sense.

The American sentry I had been talking to had started forward "Gosh! Are you hit?" People gathered round. There was the usual fuss—"Lift him up! Where's he hit? Get his shirt open!" etc. etc. The American called for a knife to cut my shirt open. I knew that there was one in my pocket and tried to get it out, but discovered that my right arm was paralyzed. Not being in pain, I had a vague satisfaction. This ought to please my wife, I thought; she had always wanted me to be wounded, which would save me from being killed when the great battle came. It was only now that it occurred to me to wonder where I was hit, and how badly; I could feel nothing, but I was conscious that the bullet had stuck me somewhere in the front of the body. When I tried to speak I found that I had no voice, only a faint squeak, but at the second attempt I managed to ask where I was hit. In the throat, they said, Harry Webb, our stretcher- bearer had brought a bandage and one of the little bottles of alcohol they gave us for field- dressings. As they lifted me up a lot of blood poured out of my mouth, and I heard a Spaniard behind me say that the bullet had gone clean through my neck. I felt the alcohol, which at ordinary times would sting like the devil, splash on the wound as a pleasant coolness.

A personal friend, T.R. Fyvel, later wrote:

There was always a touch of Don Quixote about Orwell's knight-errantry. It was typical of his political individualism that, through accident, he joined not the the International Brigade, but the so-called 'Trotskyist' P.O.U.M., a Spanish Left-Wing opposition party later suppressed by the Spanish Communists. It was typical too, that he was wounded, not in action, but on a quiet day, through sticking his head out of a trench. But he was wounded very badly. (A bullet went through his neck) and his life was saved only by a fraction' of an inch) and by the time he came out of the hospital the P.O.U.M. was proscribed as 'counter-revolutionary.' With a number of their British I.L.P friends under arrest, Orwell and his wife had to flee for their lives into France. From his ex-perience of civil war, of death, dirt and military hospitals and prisons, Orwell returned with his faith in 'ordinary people' unimpaired, but with his eyes opened to one fact: Communist despotism could be far more ruthless than the earlier, milder tyranny which it overthrew. All of this he expressed in *Homage to Catalonia* (1938), one of the most clear-headed books to come out of the Spanish Civil War, honestly and beautifully written, but which, partly because it was a book of the still unfashionable non-Communist Left, partially because this was Orwell's fate, sold only a few hundred copies over the next year or so.

He received electrotherapy for his neck wound and was deemed unfit for further service. His time in the Spanish Civil war was over.

Back in England, his health collapsed—again. In March, 1938, he was admitted to the Preston Hall Sanatorium, in Kent and diagnosed—initially—with tuberculosis.

Homage to Catalonia would not have fit Victor Gollancz's publishing house. Instead, Orwell and his agent turned to the firm of Seeker and Warburg, which published it, and later, *Animal Farm* and *1984*.

In George Orwell: The Road to 1984, Peter Lewis wrote:

> He finished *Homage to Catalonia* in January, 1938, and it was published in April while the war was still in the balance. Despite its brilliant reporting and important political analysis, "it caused barely a ripple on the political pond," in the words of Fredric Warburg. Of 1,500 copies printed, 683 were solid the first six months and thereafter only a trickle. When Orwell died in 1950, there were still copies of the first edition lying unsold in the warehouse. Orwell had not even earned the 150 (pound) advance on his royalties.

Only after Orwell's death was *Homage to Catalonia* acknowledged to be one of the most influential and significant books ever written about the Spanish Civil War.

Animal Farm—1945

His next book, written between November, 1943 and February, 1944, brought him international fame—it was in fact, a perfect combination of propaganda and art, philosophy and fable: *Animal Farm*, first published in 1945.

Orwell has seen Stalinist Communism up close in Spain and believed it to be a brutal dictatorship, built on terror.

How did Orwell conceive of the plot for this, which can be read as both a fable and a cautionary political tale? A leap of insight which writers sometimes find to their great benefit—and often to their surprise. In a Preface, Orwell writes:

> … I saw a little boy, perhaps ten years old, driving a huge cart horse a long narrow path, whipping it whenever it tried to turn. It struck me that if only such animals became aware of their own strength we should have no power over them and that men exploit animals in much the same way as the rich exploit the proletariat.

And an even earlier genesis of *Animal Farm* as fable is his memory of his favorite book as a child:

> I believe *Gulliver's Travels* that meant more to me than any other book ever written. I can't remember when I first read it. I must have been eight years old as the most, and it has lived with me ever since so that I suppose a year has never passed without my re-reading at least part of it.

The plot: most of the animals on the Manor Farm have names (just as in Clement Clark Moore's "'Twas the Night before Christmas"—*on Dasher, on Dancer, on Pracer and Vixen …*")

Old Major, an old boar, summons the animals together for a meeting in which he refers to humans as "enemies." They all learn a revolutionary song, "Beasts of England." When he dies two young pigs Snowball and Napoleon become leaders and prepare others for a coming revolution (Napoleon can be read as Stalin and Snowball as Trotsky, with some elements of Lenin.) They force the drunken farmer, Mr. Jones, from the farm and rename it Animal Farm. They adopt a dictum: the "Seven Commandments of Animalism":

The seven were:

1. Whatever goes upon two legs is an enemy.
2. Whatever goes on four legs, or has wings, is a friend.
3. No animals shall wear clothes.
4. No animal shall sleep in a bed.
5. No animal shall drink alcohol.
6. No animal shall kill any other animal.
7. All animals are equal.

The most important was: *All animals are equal.*

It becomes a commune, but later Napoleon and his pigs changed the commandments:

4. No animal shall sleep in a bed *with sheets.*
5. No animal shall drink alcohol *to excess.*
6. No animal shall kill any other animal *without cause.*

And most importantly,

7. *All animals are equal but some animals are more equal than others.*

Changing the Seven Commandments of Animalism, Orwell intimated, showed how easy it was to corrupt the system.

All the incidents in his fable directly matched the Russian Revolution and its aftermath:

The revolt of the animals against Farmer Jones is Orwell's analogy with the October 1917 Bolshevik Revolution. The Battle of the Cowshed has been said to represent the allied invasion of Soviet Russia in 1918, and the defeat of the White Russians in the Russian Civil War. The pigs' rise to preeminence mirrors the rise of a Stalinist bureaucracy in the USSR, just as Napoleon's emergency of the farms' sole leader reflects Stalin's emergence. The pigs' appropriation of milk and apples for their own use, "the turning point of the story," as Orwell termed it in a letter to Dwight Macdonald, stands as an analogy for the crushing of the left-wing Kronstadt revolt against the Bolsheviks, and the difficult efforts of the animals to build the windmill suggest the various Five Year Plans. The puppies controlled by Napoleon parallel the nurture of the secret police in the Stalinist structure, and the pigs' treatment of the other animals on the farm recalls the internal terror faced by the populace in the 1930s. In chapter seven, when the animals confess their nonexistent crimes and are killed, Orwell directly alludes to the purges, confessions and show trails of the late 1930s. These contributed to Orwell's conviction that the Bolshevik revolution had been corrupted and the Soviet system became rotten.

Orwell sought nothing less than a massive satire on the Stalinist system; to destroy the myth of Soviet superiority.

Then the unthinkable happened. Orwell's wife Eileen entered a hospital March 29, 1945 for a routine operation to remove uterine tumors. Routine, so very routine. But she died under the anesthetic. His subsequent death, alone and a 46 was tragic; her death was equally tragic. When she died she was not yet 40.

Orwell was so stricken he seldom spoke of her death. And that left him as a single parent take care of son Richard, whom Orwell and his wife had adopted.

Orwell and his agent had the same problems publishing *Animal Farm* that they experienced with his previous books. Various publishing firms in England, including Orwell's previous publisher Victor Gollancz, rejected it; other publishers in England and the United States were skeptical of the premise of the book—was it too anti-Soviet at that time? (It is perhaps apocryphal that one American publishing firm was said to have rejected it because "Americans won't read books about animals.")

Animal Farm was published August 17, 1945, less than five full months after Eileen's death; it achieved substantial recognition with the advent of the Cold War, which began in 1947, when the Truman Doctrine offered economic aid to countries threatened by Communism; the Cold War did not end until 1989, with the fall of Communism in eastern Europe, and finally in 1991 when the Soviet Union collapsed. *Animal Farm* became Orwell's first real financial—and critical—international success. Then came his masterwork.

1984—published in 1949

For many thousands—perhaps millions of readers—who came to *1984*, it has remained a remarkable example of the *sui generis* in literature. And for as many who first read it decades ago—including the author—it remains as vivid and remarkable as the day it was first read.

For those readers, with no antecedents or any *genetic history* to follow, it has remained superbly iconic; standing by itself in twentieth-century literature.

But … but … writers borrow from each other all the time. John Steinbeck's *Tortilla Flat* (1939) is an exact chapter-by-chapter retelling of the Knights of the Round Table saga. It is said that Truman Capote based his best-seller *In Cold Blood,* 1966, on a previous book, *A Murder in Paradise* by Richard Gehman, published in 1954. (The murder in Gehman's book occurred in Paradise, Pennsylvania, near Lancaster.) And there are countless other examples, recognized or unrecognized by readers.

Consider these paragraphs by Paul Owen:

> It is a book in which one man, living in a totalitarian society a number of years in the future, gradually finds himself rebelling against the dehumanizing forces of an omnipotent, omniscient dictator. Encouraged by a woman who seems to represent the political and sexual freedom of the pre-revolutionary era (and with whom he sleeps in an ancient house that is one of the few manifestations of a former world), he writes down his thoughts of rebellion—perhaps rather imprudently—as a 24-hour clock ticks in his grim, lonely flat. In the end, the system discovered both the man and the woman, and after a period of physical and mental trauma the protagonist discovers he loves the state that has oppressed him throughout, and betrays his fellow rebels.
>
> The story is intended as a warning against and prediction of the natural conclusions of totalitarianism.
>
> This is a description of George Orwell's *Nineteen Eighty-Four* …. But it is also the plot of Yevgeny Zamyatin's *We,* a Russian novel originally published in English in 1924.
>
> Orwell's novel is consistently acclaimed as one of the finest of the last 100 years … .and it remains a constant bestseller. Should it alter our respect for it that Orwell borrowed much of his plot, the outlines of three of his central figures, and the progress of the book's dramatic arc from an earlier work?

And, Owen writes:

The characters in *We* are numbers rather than named: its Winston Smith is D-503 and its Julia 1-330. Its Big Brother is known as the Benefactor, a more human figure than Orwell's almost mythical dictator, who at one point phones D-503 ("D-503? Ah … You're speaking to the Benefactor. Report to me immediately!"). Where Orwell's apartments come complete with an all-seeing "telescreen."

Zamyatin's buildings are simply made of glass, allowing each of the residents—and the "Guardians" who police them—to see in whenever they want. We's Airstrip One, or Oceania, is called OneState. Instead of puzzling over $2+2=5$, its lead character is disturbed by the square root of -1.

… and …

So does it natter that Orwell borrowed plot and characters from an earlier book? After all, it seems clear that he made superior work of literature from them. Nineteen Eighty-Four's importance comes not so much from its plot as from its immense cultural impact, which was recognized almost immediately when it won the 357 (pound) Partisan Review prize for that year's most significant contribution to literature, and which has continued to this day. Most of the aspects and ideas of the novel that still resonate so strongly are his own: newspeak, doublethink, thoughtcrime, The Thought Police, Room 101; the extreme use of propaganda, censorship and surveillance; the rewriting of history; labels and slogans that mean the opposite of what they say; the role for Britain implied in the name Airstrip One. References to these things pervade all levels of our culture.

In addition, unlike *We, Nineteen Eighty-Four* is written with expert control in an accessible style about a world recognizably our own, and its twists of plot—including the existence (or not) of the Brotherhood resistance movement—are gripping, sophisticated and convincing. The dark, pessimistic tone of *Nineteen Eighty-Four* is also all Orwell's.

If any aspect of *We* takes the shine off *Nineteen Eighty-Four*, it's that Orwell lifted that powerful ending—Winston's complete, willing capitulation to the forces and ideals of the astute—from Zamyatin. It's a wonderful, wrenching twist, in both books, and a perfect conclusion, though *We* and *Nineteen Eighty-Four* differ slightly in the fate of the female dissident: 1-330 is killed without giving up her beliefs, whereas Julia is broken in the same way as Winston.

Perhaps *We* deserves more recognition than it has had, but if *Nineteen Eighty-Four* had never existed, it is extremely doubtful Zamyatin's book would have come to fill the unique place Orwell's work now occupies. *Nineteen Eighty-Four* is an almanac of all the political ideas no "right thinking" person would ever want their government to countenance, and the word Orwellian has come to signify a badge of shame intended to shut down any movement in that direction—with an imperfect record of success.

So Orwell "westernized" We—taking it to London, not as a prediction but as a warning:

don't let this happen here.

For journalists, a book or article beginning is called the *lede* (pronounced *leed*). Orwell's *lede* is in *1984* is one of the most memorable in literature:

It was a bright cold day in April, and the clocks were striking thirteen.

In *1984* there are three world powers, constantly at war with each other. Oceania, the United States which absorbed the United Kingdom, and allies; Eurasia, the Soviet Union and allies and Eastasia, China and its allies. Alliances shift, sometimes quite suddenly and bewilderingly.

In London, Winston Smith is a minor functionary, working for the Party. Surveillance is constant. The Party's leader, Big Brother is on billboards and everywhere else. The slogan *Big Brother is Watching You* is everywhere. There is no escaping Big Brother.

The party prohibits free expression, free thought, any effort to be an individual and even prohibits sex. The Party has crafted its own history and is working to implement its own language *Newspeak*. Bad is now *not good*. If the party can control language it can control history and behavior.

Smith works at the Ministry of Truth, (Minitrue) which works on historical revisionism; changing history to reflect the party line. Revisions are explained as fixing misquotations, but are, in fact, outright lies and forgeries. The Ministry of Truth destroys historical documents; if a document does not exist, there is no proof The Party is lying.

Smith knows how the Ministry of Truth is distorting history; he lives a shabby life in "Victory Mansions," subsisting on black bread, synthetic meals and "Victory gin. "

Telescreens are everywhere—flat screens inset into homes and flats, which constantly broadcast Party victories and achievements, but also can also *see into* everyone's homes and apartments—they can observe everyone and anyone, at any time.

Smith assumes the telescreens can *observe everyone all the time*.

The telescreens especially observe those who might challenge the Party's authority. Even children are encouraged by the Party to inform on their parents, relatives or friends.

There is no escape from the constant surveillance by the Party.

Everything about the Party is a black reversal:

- The Ministry of Peace (Minipax) deals with war;
- The Ministry of Plenty (Miniplenty) deals with starvation;
- The Ministry of Love (Miniluv) deals with law and order, which means torture and brainwashing;
   … and
- The Ministry of Truth (MiniTrue) which deals with propaganda.

Smith begins writing a journal, which he knows is a death warrant. He records his feelings about Julia, an acquaintance who works in the same office complex.

Julia subsequently hands him a note—she is in love with him. They meet upstairs above an antique shop, where Smith bought his journal. They assume there are no telescreens in the old shabby building, but they are betrayed by the owner of the shop who is a member of the Thought Police.

Smith is taken to the Ministry of Love and is interrogated by O'Brien, who Smith knows; O'Brien is also a member of the Party, but in a position slightly above Smith's.

O'Brien subjects Smith to electroshock treatments and tells Smith that he can be "cured" of his insanity—his hatred of the Party—through conditioning. Smith "confesses" to "crimes" he has committed.

He is eventually taken to Room 101—the ultimate location for re-indoctrination—brainwashing.

It is every citizen's fear about the Party.

Smith betrays Julia when a wire cage with hungry rats inside is placed over his head.

"Do it to Julia," he says, in abject panic.

Later he meets Julia on the street, in a crowd—she admits she betrayed him, in Room 101, faced with the same wire cage with the hungry rats.

Eventually he is content to sit in a cafe, remembering a rare happy time with his family, but now believes it to be false.

He is content to love Big Brother.

Nazi rockets continued to rain down on London and elsewhere: one rocket fell near his flat; Orwell needed a safe place to take his son Richard, whom he and his wife had adopted, and finish his novel. He had contributed articles, essays, opinion pieces and reviews to a wide variety of British publications over the years—always earning little more than a meager income. He had worked for David Astor, publisher of *The Observer*. Astor offered him a place to stay:

> His family owned an estate on the remote Scottish island of Jura, next to Islay. There was a house, Barnhill, seven miles outside Ardlussa at the remote tip of this rocky finger of heather in the Inner Hebrides. Initially Astor offered it to Orwell as a holiday.
>
> In May, 1946, Orwell, still picking up the shattered pieces of his life, took the train for the long and arduous journey to Jura. He told his friend Arthur Koestler that it was "almost like stocking up (a) ship for a arctic voyage."

It was a moonscape; it has been described as:

> … mountainous, bare and infertile, covered largely by vast areas of blanket bog, hence its small population. In a list of the islands of Scotland, ranked by size Jura comes in eighth, whereas by population it comes in thirty-first. Jura, in ancient Norse, means Deer Island.

The house in Jura (biographer Jeffrey Meyers calls this his "Jurrasic Period") was scarcely more than just an isolated shelter to live and finish *1984.*

The Jura residents then knew him by his real name: Eric Blair. "a tall cadaverous, sad-looking man, worrying about how to cope on his own … a specter in the mist, a gaunt figure in oil-skins." His sister Avril arrived to manage things. It was a godsend to Orwell.

His health was precarious before his trek to Jura, but he kept on, doggedly working on his book.

Then, an accident, a disaster for Orwell. In a boat with Arvil, Richard and some friends, an infamous whirlpool capsized the boat. Son Richard remembered being "bloody cold." They were rescued by others. He did not go to a doctor after that incident.

Orwell went on.

Within two months he was seriously ill.

He kept on.

In *Why I Write,* he said:

> Writing a book is a horrible, exhausting struggle, like a long bout of some painful illness. One would never undertaken such a thing if one were not driven by some demon whom one can neither resist or (sic) understand. For all one knows that demon is the same instinct that makes baby squall for attention. And yet it is also true that one can write nothing readable unless one constantly struggles to efface one's personality. Good prose is like a window pane.

He kept on. At Christmas, 1947, he told friends that he had been diagnosed with tuberculosis. Then, in March, 1948, he received word from his publisher Fred Warburg: "it's necessary from the point of view of your literary career to get it (done) by the end of the year and indeed earlier if possible."

Get it done by the end of 1948. Or sooner. While battling tuberculosis.

Robert McCrum writes:

> It was a desperate race against time. Orwell's health was deteriorating, the "unbelievable bad" manuscript needs retyping, and the December deadline was looming. Warburg promised to help, as did Orwell's agent. At cross-purposes over possible typists, they somehow contrived to make a bad situation infinitely worse. Orwell, feeling beyond help, followed his ex-public schoolboy's instincts; he would go it alone.

In fact, Orwell eventually worked on his project in bed, physically unable to get up.

The "unbelievable bad" manuscript: writers with some experience, who write (these days) a page on a screen and then print it out for proofreading, might be dismayed (or worse) to find three, four or five typescript errors on a page. *Nineteen Eighty-Four: The Facsimile* (edition) shows typescript changes *on every line of every page. Many manuscript pages are simply garble. That's how a masterpiece is revised and completed, but the hardship cost him dearly.*

McCrum suggests—or believes—that finishing the book with his health very much at risk cost Orwell his life.

The manuscript reached Orwell's publisher in mid-December. Fred Warburg recognized its importance immediately: it was, he said, "among the most terrifying books I have ever read."

Orwell entered a TB sanitarium.

Nineteen Eighty-Four was published June 8, 1949 and was instantly recognized as a masterpiece.

Winston Churchill (Orwell, who admired Churchill, named his protagonist Winston after Churchill) said he had read it—twice.

What had Orwell done in his book? He had transformed *We*—westernized it as a warning—and had made an indelible impression on readers for generations.

All the incidents and anecdotes in *Animal Farm* directly match the Russian Revolution and its aftermath.

How extensively did Orwell use the same techniques in *1984*? Consider these key elements:

- **Big Brother:** during World War Two in London, J.M. Bennett had a company, Bennett's, which offered correspondence courses for students. He appeared on billboards with the slogan "Let me be your father." Later, after he died, his son took over and the billboard slogan became "Let me be your big brother."

Orwell worked for the British Broadcasting Company, the B.B.C., during World War Two, providing propaganda for the war effort. His superior was Brendan Bracken, the Minister of Information; M.O.I. staff members referred to him as B.B.

Most tellingly, in political terms, Big Brother was most assuredly Joseph Stalin; Orwell described Big Brother as having a mustache, like Stalin.

- **Emmanuel Goldstein:** Big Brother's arch-nemesis said to form a underground resistance movement, The Brotherhood, and who wrote *The Theory and Practice of Oligarchial Collectivism*. Goldstein said to have been exiled by Big Brother or otherwise fled.

Leon Trotsky born October 26, 1879, joined the Bolshevik ("majority") just before the 1917 October Revolution. He ascended to top Party ranks and become one of the first seven members of the Politburo.

He served first as People's Commissar for Foreign Affairs, founder of the Red Army and became a major figure in the Bolshevik victory in the Russian Civil war.

But after a failed struggle by the left against the politics of Stalin, he was removed as Commissar for Military and Naval Affairs, January, 1925, removed from the Politburo, October, 1926, removed from the Central Committee, October, 1927, exiled to Alma-Ata, January, 1928 and exiled from the Soviet Union, February, 1929.

Trotsky was attacked in Mexico City in August 20, 1944 by Ramon Mercader, a Spanish-born NKVD agent wielding an axe handle. Trotsky died the next day; Mercader served 20 years in a Mexican prison. While in prison he was awarded an Order of Lenin by Stalin, in absentia.

The description of Goldstein with "a small goatee beard," evoked the image of Trotsky. The film of Goldstein during the Two Minute Hate is described as showing him being transformed into a bleating sheep. This same type of image was used in a propaganda film during the Kino-eye period of Soviet film, which shows Trotsky transformed into a goat. Goldstein's book is similar to Trotsky's highly critical analysis of the USSR, *The Revolution Betrayed,* published in 1936.

Leon Trotsky's birth name was Lev Davidovich Bronstein.

- **Oceania, Eurasia, Eastasia.** International spheres of influence were suggested by the Tehran Conference, November-December, 1943.

- **Sudden and dramatic shifts in alliances between Oceania, Eurasia and Eastasia;** based on the Nazi-Soviet Peace Pact and the subsequent and unexpected invasion of Russia by Hitler in Operation Barbarossa.

- **"... the clocks were striking thirteen."** The 24-hour military clock was in universal use: thirteen is 1 p.m.

Orwell's remarkable *neologisms*—newly coined words or phrases—have long been a part of common usage and culture:

- **Big Brother**—any dictatorial figure, real or mythical;

- **Thought Police—Thought Crime.** (Thinkpol in *1984)* . So unlikely as to be unbelievable? Even in *1984*?

  The Thought Police is based on the NKVD, which arrested people at random for "anti-Soviet remarks."

  In the early twentieth century—specifically in 1911 —the Empire of Japan established the Special Higher Police, a political police known as the *Shiso Keisho,* the Thought Police, who investigated and controlled native political groups whose ideologies were considered a threat to the public order of the countries colonized by Japan. In contemporary usage the term *Thought Police* often refers to the actual or perceived enforcement of ideological orthodoxy in the political life of a society.

- **Room 101.** The ultimate torture chamber; in *1984,* every prisoner's worse fears about the Party, where a cage of rats was fitted over Winston Smith's head, to force him to confess to anti-Party "crimes." Orwell worked in a room 101 for the British Broadcasting Company, during World War Two, where he detested the propaganda work he was doing.

- **Unpersons.** People who are erased from history.

  During the Stalinist years, photographs which included officials who had fallen from favor were doctored to eliminate their images. Examples: Lavrentiy Beria—when he fell from power in 1953, and was subsequently executed, institutions and libraries which had encyclopedias with' his picture were sent an article about the Bering Strait and told to paste it over the Beria material. And Nikolai Yezhov, who was shown in a photo with Stalin in the mid-1930s: when he was executed in 1940, his image was airbrushed out of the photo. They had become unpersons.

- **Doublethink.** The ability to hold two contradictory concepts in mind at the same time—and to ignore the fact that they *are* contradictory.

- **Doublespeak** and **groupthink,** variations of doublethink. **Facecrime,** to inadvertently reveal anti-Big Brother emotions, which would lead to arrest or worse.

- **Memory hole**—when facts and history are deleted and permanently lost, they go down the memory hole.

  … and finally …

- **Orwellian**—any reference to, or description of, a dictator or a totalitarian or dictatorial society.

* * *

And, a now-infamous wrought-iron Orwellian sign/ slogan, over a gate at Auschwitz 1, the largest of the Nazi death camps read: **ARBEIT MACHT FREI**, roughly translated as *Work is freedom* or *Work makes you free.*

("The sign was also used at other death camps.") Prisoners at Auschwitz and other Nazi death camps well knew they would likely die by overwork or starve to death. Prisoners with metal-working skills made the sign and in a subtle act of defiance, the B in ARBEIT was set upside down. It remains so to this day.

* * *

And another remarkably Big Brother statement—with the logic of 2 + 2 = 5—occurred during the Vietnam war: **We had to destroy the village to save it.**

Zafar Sobhan summarized the story in *The Guardian:*

> Ben Tre is a city in the Mekong Delta in Vietnam, made famous by the statement of an unnamed US army officer to AP correspondent Peter Arnett in the aftermath

of the crippling aerial assault it suffered at the hands of the US Air Force during the Vietnam war: *It became necessary to destroy the town to save it.* (Italics added.)

The quote has since become distorted in the popular imagination and became immortalized in the familiar form used as the title this piece, but, either way, it still stands as a classic statement of the folly of war and as a monument to the depths to which human idiocy can sink when we are blinded by our belief that we are in the right and the other side is in the wrong.

* * *

Outside the remarkable neologisms in *1984*, Orwell was the first to substantially establish the concept of the **Cold War.** The article, "George Orwell and the origins of the term 'cold war'" states:

> On 19 October 1945 George Orwell used the term cold war in his essay "You and the Atomic Bomb," speculating on the repercussions of the atomic age which had begun two months before when the United States bombed Hiroshima and Nagasaki in Japan. In this article, Orwell considered the social and political implications of a "state which was at once unconquerable and in a permanent state of 'cold war' with its neighbors."
>
> This wasn't the first time the phrase *cold war* was used in English (it had been used to describe certain policies of Hitler in 1938), but it seems to have been the first time it was applied to the conditions that arose in the aftermath of World War II. Orwell's essay speculates on the geopolitical impact of the advent of a powerful weapon so expensive and difficult to produce that it was attainable by only a handful of nations, anticipating "the prospects of two or three monstrous super-states, each possessed of

a weapon by which millions of people can be wiped out in a few seconds, dividing the world between them," and concluding that such a situation is likely "to put an end to large-scale wars the coast of prolonging indefinitely 'a *peace that is no peace.'*"

Within years, some of the developments anticipated by Orwell had emerged. *The Cold War* (often with capital letters) came to refer specifically two the prolonged state of hostility, short of direct armed conflict, which existed between the Soviet bloc and Western powers after the Second World War. The term was popularized by the American journalist Walter Lippmann, who made it the title of a series of essays he published in 1947 in response to U.S. diplomat George Kennan's "Mr. X" article, which had advocated the policy of "containment." To judge by debate in the House of Commons the following year (as cited by the *Oxford English Dictionary*), this use of the term *Cold War* was initially regarded as an Americanism: "The British government ... should recognize that the 'cold war' as the Americans call it, is on in earnest, that the third world war has, in fact, begun." Soon though, the term was in general use.

* * *

Orwell had graphically and dramatically shown the evils and cruelty of totalitarianism in *1984* in ways *Animal Farm* did not; for some readers the Russian Revolution references in *Animal Farm* were too obscure to be noticed or understood (re: the apocryphal American publisher who said "Americans don't buy animal books").

In October, 1949, in his room at University College Hospital, Orwell married Sonia Brownell. It was a moment of happiness— but only a fleeting moment.

Orwell suffered a massive hemorrhage January 21, 1950. He died alone, at 46.

In *Churchill and Orwell: The Fight for Freedom,* Thomas E. Ricks writes: "When he was alive, his book sales were measured in the hundreds and thousands. Since his death an estimated 50 million copies of his books have been sold."

By 1989, *1984* had been translated into 65 languages throughout the world.

And sales spiked to the top of the best-seller lists with the advent of the Trump administration.

A half million copies were printed in January, 2017 .

from *1984*

It was a bright cold day in April, and the clocks were striking thirteen. Winston Smith, his chin muzzled into his breast in an effort to escape the vile wind, slipped quickly through the glass doors of Victory Mansions though not quickly enough to prevent a swirl of gritty dust from entering along with him.

The hallway smelt of boiled cabbage and old rag mats. At one end of it a colored poster, far too large for indoor display, had been tacked to the wall. It depicted simply an enormous face, more than a meter wide; the face of a man about forty- five, with a heavy black mustache and ruggedly handsome features. Winston made for the stairs. It was no use trying the lift. Even at the best of times it was seldom working and at present the electric current was cut off during daylight hours. It was part of the economy drive in preparation for Hate Week.

* * *

The Ministry of Truth—Minitrue in Newspeak—was startlingly different from any other object in sight. It was an enormous pyramidal structure of glittering white concrete, soaring up terrace after terrace, three hundred meters into the air. From where Winston stood it was just possible to read, picked out on its white face in elegant lettering, the three slogans of the Party:

WAR IS PEACE
FREEDOM IS SLAVERY
IGNORANCE IS STRENGTH

… the question was …

In the beginning pages, if you recall, the question was: in any of his books, diary entries, essays, notes, plans or conversations with his wife, friends or colleagues, did Orwell ever think of journeying to America to write a De Tocqueville-type update? A *1984*-in-America project, a matching volume or an American sequel to *1984*?

The answer is: he had little or no curiosity or interest in America; never expressed any interest in traveling to America. He came back to England after suffering the neck wound in the Spanish Civil War that—for a fraction of an inch—would have killed him.

He had focused on Fascism and Communism while in Spain.

His health was suspect for much of his adult life; he began working on *Animal Farm,* then *1984,* after moving to the desolate moonscape of Jura.

An American sequel to *1984* was never in his thoughts—it was a desperate race against time—his looming collapse—to complete *1984.*

… a conundrum …

So now we have a conundrum, defined as a confusing or difficult problem: if Orwell had no interest in America, no curiosity, no time in his life left after returning to England following his stint in the Spanish Civil War—no time to focus after *Animal Farm* except desperately striving to complete *1984,* why is the title of this book *Orwell in America*?

Simply stated, *1984* was, and is, not a prediction, it is a *warning:*

> *Don't let this happen here …*

Not in England, not in America, nor elsewhere in the world.

He emphasized in horrific detail, four areas: constant warfare; constant surveillance; prohibited sex and torture.

So the key question is: how close are we now, in America, 70 years gone now since *1984* was first published, how close are we to Orwell's warnings?

The answers are: too close.

Too close in constant warfare; too close in constant surveillance; in laws against sexual freedom, and in state-authorized torture.

Readers in 1949, encountering *1984* for the first time, saw it as horrific—never to be believed—dystopian science fiction. Readers today—especially high school, college and university students—read it as simple fact:

It's true. It's all true. Now. It's all true.

So this book examines how Orwell's dystopian novel has come true in America—the constant warfare, the unrelenting surveillance, possible/probable laws against sexual freedom and state-approved torture.

And in one area—that was 'way beyond Orwell's imagination, well beyond Big Brother.

That's chapter nine.

Orwell in America

3

Constant Warfare

Winston could not definitely remember a time when
his country had not been at war …
—1984

"I can't remember a time when
our country hasn't been at war in Afghanistan."
—any 18-year-old American

Warfare has been in America's DNA since before the earliest years of the republic. In fact, citizens—and even some historians—may never have known, how many wars the United States has been involved in, since 1775: international; large; smaller or skirmishes now simply forgotten.

These are the wars involving the United States (and allies) from 1775 onward. (Opponents on right.)

These lists are simply that: listings of beginning and end dates; there is no calculus here of the year-by-year, decade-by-decade, war-by-war, cost in the permanently wounded, shattered lives, suffering, deaths, mourning … the calculus of the human heart.

The losses—deaths in the American Civil War alone were commonly thought to be 620,000; new estimates now place that number at 750,000.

18th Century Wars

American Revolutionary War—1775-1783

United States	Great Britain
France	German mercenaries
other allies	other allies

Result: Victory, Treaty of Paris, 1783, Independence from Great Britain.

Cherokee-American Wars—1776-1796

(Part of the American Indian Wars)

United States	Cherokee

Result: Victory.

Northwest Indian War—1785-1793

(Part of the American Indian Wars)

United States	Great Britain
Chickasaw	Choctaw

Result: Victory, Treaty of Greenville, Withdrawal of the British.

Shays' Rebellion—1766-1787

United States	anti-government protestors

Result: Victory.

Whiskey Rebellion—1791-1794

United States	Frontier tax protesters

Result: Victory.

Quasi-War—1798-1800

United States	France
Great Britain	Guadeloupe

Result: Victory, end of French privateer attacks on American shipping.

19th Century Wars

First Barbary War—1801-1805

    United States   Eyalet of Tripolitania

    Sweden   Sultanate of Morocco

Result: Victory, peace treaty.

German Coast Uprising—1811

    United States   Rebel slaves supported by Haiti

Result: Victory, suppression and later trials.

Tecumseh's War—1811

(Part of the American Indian Wars and the War of 1812)

    United States   Tecumseh's Confederacy

Result: Victory, peace treaty.

War of 1812

    United States   United Kingdom

    Cherokee nation   British North America

    Creek allies   Tecumseh's Confederacy

Result: stalemate.

Creek War—1813-1814

(Part of the American Indian Wars and the War of 1812)

    United States   Red Stick Creek

    Lower Creeks

    Cherokee Nation

    Choctaw

Result: Victory, Creek forced to cede 23 million acres of their territory to the United States in the treaty of Fort Jackson.

Second Barbary War—1815

    United States   Regency of Algiers

Result: Victory, peace treaty

First Seminole War—1817-1818

    United States   Seminole

Result: Victory, Spain cedes Spanish Florida to the United States.

Texas-Indian Wars—1820-1875

    United States   Comanche

    Republic of Texas

    Spain

    Mexico

Result: Victory.

Arikara War—1823

    United States   Arikara

Result: Partial victory.

Aegean Sea Anti-Privacy Operations of the United States—1825-1828

    United States   Greek pirates

Result: Victory.

Winnebago War—1827

(Part of the American Indian Wars)

    United States   Prairie La Crosse

                                Ho-Chucks

Result: Victory.

First Sumatran expedition—1832

    United States   Chiefdom of Kuala Batee

    Netherlands

Result: Victory.

Black Hawk War—1832

(Part of the American Indian Wars)

    United States   Black Hawks

    Ho-Chuck   British Band Ho-Chuck

    Menominee   Potawatomi

    Dakota

    Potawatomi

Result: Victory.

Second Seminole War—1835-1842

    United States   Seminole

Result: Victory. 3,800 Seminoles transported to the Indian territory; 300 remain in the Everglades.

Second Sumatran expedition—1838

    United States   Chiefdom of Kuala Batee

    Netherlands

Result: Victory.

Aroostook War—1838

    United States   United Kingdom

                                 British North America

Result: Compromise.

Ivory Coast Expedition—1842

    United States   Ivory Coast

Result: Victory

Mexican-American War—1848

    United States   Mexico

    California Republic

Result: Victory

Cayuse War—1855

    United States   Cayuse

Result: Victory

Apache Wars—1851-1900

    United States   Apache

                              Ute

                              Yavapai

Result: Victory.

Puget Sound War—1855-1856

(Part of the American Indian Wars)

    United States   Nisqually

    Snoqualmie   Muckleshoot

                              Puyallup

                              Klickitat

                              Haida

                              Tlingit

Result: Victory.

First Fiji Expedition—1855

    United States   Fiji

Result: Victory.

Rogue River Wars—1855-1856

    United States   Rogue River people

Result: Victory.

Third Seminole War—1855-1858

    United States   Seminole

Result: Victory. By the late 1850s, most Seminoles forced leave their land; a few hundred remained deep in the Everglades.

Yakima War—1855-1858

    United States   Yakama

                                Walla Walla tribe

                                Umatilla tribe

                                Nez Perce tribe

                                Cayuse tribe

Result: Peace treaty.

Second Opium War—1856-1859

    United States   Qing Dynasty

    British Empire

    French Empire

Result: Treaty.

Utah War—1858

    United States   Deseret/Utah Mormons

Result: Compromise.

Navajo Wars—1866

    United States   Navajo

Result: Victory.

Second Fiji Expedition—1859

    United States   Fiji

Result: Victory.

John Brown's raid on Harper's Ferry—1859

United States   Abolitionist insurgents
Result: Victory.

First and Second Cortina War—1859-1861

United States   Cortinista bandits
Confederate states
Mexico
Result: Victory.

Palute War

United States   Paiute
                                 Shoshone
                                 Bannock

Result: Victory.

American Civil War—1861-1865

United States   Confederate States
Result: Victory.

Yavapai Wars—1861-1875

United States   Yavapai
                                 Apache
                                 Yuma
                                 Mohave

Result: Victory.

Dakota War of 1862 1862

United States   Dakota Sioux
Result: Victory.

Colorado War—1863-1865

United States   Cheyenne

Arapaho

Sioux

Result: Victory.

Shimonoseki War—1863-1864

British Empire   Choshu Domain

United States

Dutch Empire

French Empire

Result: Victory.

Snake War—1864-1868

United States   Paiute

Bannock

Shoshone

Result: Victory

Powder River War—1865

United States   Sioux

Cheyenne

Arapaho

Result: Stalemate

Red Cloud's War—1866-1868

United States   Lakota

Result: Defeat; legal control of Powder River Country ceded to
Native Americans.

Formosa Expedition—1867

United States   Paiwan

Result: Defeat; American withdrawal after commander killed.

Comanche Campaign—1867-1875

United States   Cheyenne

Arapaho

Comanche

Kiowa

Result: Victory

United States expedition to Korea—1871

United States   Joseon Dynasty

Result: Victory.

Modoc War—1872-1873

United States   Modoc

Result: Victory.

Red River War—1874-1875

United States   Cheyenne

Arapaho

Comanche

Result: Victory; ends the Texas-Indian Wars.

Las Cuevas War—1875

United States   Mexico

Result: Victory.

Great Sioux War of 1876—1876-1877

United States   Lakota

Dakota Sioux

Northern Cheyenne

Arapaho

Result: Victory.

Buffalo Hunters' War—1876-1877

    United States   Comanche

                                       Apache

Result: Victory.

Nez Perce War—1877

    United States   Nez Perce

                                       Palouse

Result: Victory

Bannock War—1878

    United States   Bannock

                                       Shoshone

                                       Palute

Result: Victory

Cheyenne War—1878-1879

    United States   Cheyenne

Result: Victory.

Sheepeater Indian War—1879

    United States   Shoshone

Result: Victory.

Victorio's War—1879-1881

    United States   Apache

Result: Victory.

White River War—1879-1880

    United States   Ute

Result: Victory.

Pine Ridge Campaign—1890-1891

United States   Sioux
Result: Victory.

Garza Revolution—1891-1893

United States   Garzistas
Mexico
Result: Victory

Yaqui Wars—1896-1918

United States   Yaqui
Mexico   Pima
                                  Opata

Result: Victory.

Second Samoan Civil War—1898-1899

Samoa   Mataafans
United States   Germany
Result: Compromise.

Spanish-American War 1898

United States   Spain
Cuban Revolutionaries   Cuba
Filipino Revolutionaries   Guam
                                  Philipines
                                  Puerto Rico

Result: Victory.

Philippine-American War—1899-1902

1899-1902	1899-1902
United States	Philippine Republic
Military Government	Negros Republic
	Zamboanga Republic

1902-1906	1902-1906
United States	Tagalog Republic
Civilian Government	Irrenconcilables

Result: Victory.

Moro Revolution—1899-1913

United States	Moro
	Remnants of the Sulu
	Sultanate

Result: Victory.

Boxer Rebellion—1899-1901

United Kingdom	Righteous Harmony Society (Boxers)
Russia	China
Japan	
France	
United States	
Germany	
Italy	
Austria-Hungary	

Result: Victory.

20th Century Wars

Crazy Snake Rebellion—1909
>   United States   Creek
Result: Victory.

Border War—1910-1919
>   United States   Mexico
>   Germany

Result: Victory.

Negro Rebellion—1912
>   Cuba   Cuban PIC
>   United States
Result: Victory.

Occupation of Nicaragua—1912-1913
>   United States   Nicaraguan Liberal
>   Sandinistas
>   Nicaragua
Result: Victory.

Bluff War—1914-1915
>   United States   Ute
>   Paiute

Result: Victory.

Occupation of Veracruz—1914
>   United States   Mexico
Result: Victory.

Occupation of Haiti—1915-1934

United States   Haitian Rebels

Haiti

Result: Victory.

Occupation of the Dominican Republic—1916-1924

United States   Dominican Republic

Result: Victory.

World War I—1914-1918

France   Germany

British Empire   Austria-Hungary

Russia   Ottoman Empire

United States   Bulgaria

China

Italy

Japan

Serbia

Montenegro

Romania

Belgium

Greece

Portugal

Brazil

Result: Victory.

Russian Civil War—1918-1920

White Movement   Russian SFSR

British Empire   Far Eastern Republic

Japan   Latvian SSR

Czechoslovakia   Ukranian SSR

Greece   Commune of Estonia

Poland   Mongolia Communities
United States
France
Romania
Serbia
Italy
China
Result: Defeat

Last Indian Uprising—1923

United States   Ute
                            Paiute

Result: Victory

World War II—1939-1945

Soviet Union   Germany
United States   Japan
United Kingdom   Italy
China   Hungary
France   Romania
Poland   Bulgaria
Canada   Finland
Australia   Thailand
New Zealand   Manchukuo
India   Mengjiang
South Africa   Croatia
Yugoslavia   Slovakia
Greece
Denmark
Norway
Netherlands
Belgium

Luxembourg

Czechoslovakia

Brazil

Mexico

Ethiopia

Mongolia

Philippines

Viet Minh

KLA

Albania

Result: Victory; emergence of the United States and Russia as superpowers, beginning of the Cold War.

Korean War—1950-1953

South Korea	North Korea
United States	China
United Kingdom	Soviet Union
Australia	
Belgium	
Canada	
France	
Philippines	
Columbia	
Ethiopia	
Greece	
Luxembourg	
Netherlands	
New Zealand	
South Africa	
Thailand	
Turkey	

Result: Stalemate.

Operation Ajax—1953

House of Pahlavi   Government of Iran
United States
United Kingdom

Result: Victory.

Laotian Civil War—1953-1975

Kingdom of Laos	Pathet Lao
United States	North Vietnam (support)
South Vietnam	Soviet Union
Thailand (support)	China
Philippines	
Taiwan	

Result: Defeat.

Lebanon Crisis—1958

Lebanon	Lebanese Opposition
United States	INM; LCP; PSP

Result: Victory.

Bay of Pigs Invasion—1961

CDRF	Cuba
United States	

Result: Defeat.

Vietnam War—1965-1973, 1975

South Vietnam	North Vietnam
United States	Viet Cong
South Korea	Khmer Rouge
Australia	Pathet Lao
New Zealand	China
Thailand	

Philippines
Khmer Republic
Kingdom of Laos
Result: Defeat.

Communist Insurgency in Thailand—1965-1983

Thailand	Communist Party of Thailand (until July, 1967)
Taiwan	Pathet Lao
United States	Khmer Rouge (until 1978) (support)
Malaysia	North Vietnam (until 1976)
	Vietnam (from 1976)
	Peoples Republic of China (1971-1978)
	Malayan Communist Party
	North Korea

Result: Victory.

Korean DMZ Conflict—1966-1969

South Korea	North Korea
United States	

Result: Victory.

Dominican Civil War—1965-1966

Dominican Loyalists	Dominican Constitutionalists
United States	
Inter-American	
Peace Force:	
Brazil	
Paraguay	
Nicaragua	

Costa Rica
El Salvador
Honduras
Result: Victory.

Insurgence in Bolivia—1966-1967

Bolivia   Ejercito de Liberation
                                 Nacional

United States
Result: Victory.

Cambodian Civil War—1967-1975

Kingdom of Cambodia   National United Front
(1967-1970)   of Kampuchea
Khmer Republic   Khmer Rouge
(1970-1975)
United States   Khmer Rumdo
South Korea (support)   Khmer Viet Minh
Australia   North Vietnam
Canada   Viet Cong (support)
France   China
India   Czechoslovakia
Thailand   Soviet Union
Result: Defeat.

War in South Zaire—1978

Zaire   Front for the National
                                 Liberation of the Congo
                                 (support)
France   Angola
Belgium   Cuba

| United States | Soviet Union |
| Morocco | |

Result: Victory.

Operation Eagle Claw—1980

| United States | Iran |

Result: Blunder.

Gulf of Sidra encounter—1981

| United States | Libya |

Result: Victory.

Lebanese Civil War—1982-1984

Lebanese Armed Forces	Lebanese National Movement
Multinational Force	Amal Movement
in Lebanon:	
United States,	Iran
France, Italy	Hezbollah
	Islamic Unification Movement
	Arab Determent Forces:
	Saudia Arabia; Sudan; UAE;
	Libya; South Yemen

Result: Defeat.

Invasion of Grenada—1983

United States	PRG of Grenada
Barbados	Cuba
Jamaica	
Antigua and Barbuda	
Dominica	
Saint Kitts and Nevis	

Sanin Lucia
Saint Vincent and the
Grenadines
Result: Victory.

Action in the Gulf of Sidra—1986
United States   Libya
Result: Victory.

Bombing of Libya—1986
United States   Libya
Result: Victory.

Tanker War—1987-1988
United States   Iran
Result: Mixed.

Tobruk Encounter—1989
United States   Libya
Result: Victory.

Invasion of Panama—1989-1990
United States   Panama
Panamanian Opposition
Result: Victory. Dictator Manuel Noriega deposed.

Gulf War—1990-1991
Kuwait   Iraq
United States
United Kingdom
Saudi Arabia
France

Canada
Egypt
Syria
Qatar
Bahrain
United Arab Emirates
Oman
Bangladesh
Result: Victory.

Iraq No-Fly Zone Enforcement—1991-2003

United States   Iraq
United Kingdom
France
Australia
Belgium
Netherlands
Saudi Arabia
Turkey
Italy
Result: Victory.

First Intervention in the Somali Civil War—1992-1995

United States   Somali National Alliance
United Kingdom
Spain
Saudi Arabia
Malaysia
Pakistan
Italy
Greece
Germany

France
Canada
Botswana
Belgium
Australia
New Zealand
Result: Mixed.

Bosnian War—1992-1995

Herzeg-Bosnia	Republika Srpska
Croatia	YPA
United States	Serbian Krajina
Belgium	Western Bosnia
Canada	FR Yugoslavia
France	
Germany	
Italy	
Luxembourg	
Netherlands	
Norway	
Portugal	
Spain	
Turkey	
United Kingdom	

Result: Stalemate.

Intervention in Haiti—1994-1995

United States	Haiti
Poland	
Argentina	

Result: Victory.

Kosovo War—1998-1999

KLA	FR Yugoslavia
AFRK	
Albania	
Croatia	
United States	
Belgium	
Canada	
Czech Republic	
Denmark	
France	
Germany	
Hungary	
Italy	
Luxembourg	
Netherlands	
Norway	
Portugal	
Poland	
Spain	
Turkey	
United Kingdom	

Result: Mixed.

Operation Infinite Reach—1998

United States	al-Qaeda
	Sudan

Results: Mixed.

21st Century Wars

Nepalese Civil War—2002-2006

Kingdom of Nepal	Communist Party of Nepal
United States	Communist of India
United Kingdom	
Belgium	
India	

Result: Defeat.

War in Afghanistan—2001-present

Afghanistan	Taliban
United States	Islamic Jihad Union
Canada	Haqqani network
United Kingdom	Allied groups: HIG; al-Qaeda; IJU
Australia	Taliban splinter groups
Croatia	IS-affiliates
Czech Republic	2001 Invasion:
Georgia	Islamic Emirate of Afghanistan
Germany	Taliban Army
Italy	Salafist extremists
Romania	055 Brigade
Spain	
Turkey	

Result: Ongoing.

Iraq War—2003-2011

United States	Ba'ath Loyalists
Iraq	Islamic State of Iraq

United Kingdom   al-Qaeda in Iraq
Australia   Mahdi Army
South Korea   Special Groups
Italy   IAI
Georgia   Anar al-Sunnah
Poland   Invasion 2001:
Spain   Iraq
Netherlands
Ukraine
Romania
Result: Mixed.

War in North-West Pakistan—2004-present

United States   Tehrik + Taliban
Pakistan   Pakistan: al-Qaeda; Lashkar-
                             e-Jhangyi; Turkish Islamic
                             Party; Tehreek-e-Nafaz-
                             e-Shariat-e-Mohammadi;
                             Daesh
Result: Ongoing.

War in Somalia—2007-present

Somalia   Al-Shabaab
United States   Hizbul Islam
United Kingdom   Daesh
Kenya   Support: Eritea
Ethiopia
AMISOM
Result: Ongoing.

Operation Ocean Shield—2009-2016

NATO: Somali pirates

United States

Malaysia

Norway

United Kingdom

New Zealand

Denmark

Netherlands

Italy

South Korea

India

Result: Victory.

American-led Intervention in Libya—2001

NATO: Libya

United States

United Kingdom

Belgium

Bulgaria

Canada

Denmark

France

Greece

Italy

Netherlands

Norway

Romania

Spain

Turkey

Sweden

Jordan
Qatar
United Arab Emirates
Result: Victory.

Lord's Resistance Army Insurgence—2011-2017

United States   Lord's Resistance Army
Uganda
DR Congo
Central African Republic
South Sudan
Result: Mixed/Ongoing.

American-led Intervention in Iraq—2014-2017

United States   Islamic State of Iraq and Syria
Iraq
Kurdistan
Australia
Belgium
Canada
Denmark
France
Germany
Jordan
Morocco
Netherlands
United Kingdom
Turkey
Iran
Hezbollah
Result: Victory.

American-led Intervention in Syria—2014-present

United States	ISIS
Syrian Democratic Forces	al-Qaeda linked groups:
Democratic Federation of	al-Nusra Front
Northern Syria	
IFB	Khorasan group
People's Protection Units	Jund al-Aqsa
Women's Protection Units	Partial support:
CJTF-OIR Members:	Qatar
United Kingdom	UAE
France	Saudi Arabia
Australia	Syria (limited encounters with US and Israel)
Canada	Supported by:
Jordan	Russia
Denmark	Iran
Netherlands	Hezbollah
Belgium	China
Lebanon	
Morocco	
Saudi Arabia	
UAE	
Qatar	
Bahrain	
Turkey	
Israel	
Free Syrian Army	
(2011-2017)	

Result: Ongoing.

Yemeni Civil War—2015-present

Hadi government	Supreme Political Council
Saudi-led Coalition: Saudi Arabia; UAE; Senegal; Sudan;	Supported by: Iran; Hezbollah; North Korea; AQAP; IS (Islamic State)-affiliated groups

Qatar (2015-2017)
minor support:
United States
France
United Kingdom
Result: Ongoing.

American Intervention in Libya—2015-present

United States	Islamic State in Libya
Libya	

Status: Ongoing.

In the 21st century wars, notice how many results are: "Ongoing" or "Mixed." Writing on the internet on March 19, 2017, Arthur Charpentier said:

> *America has been at war 93 percent of the time—222 out of 239 years since 1776,* i.e., the U.S. has only been at peace for less than 20 years total since its birth.
>
> (Italics added.)

How long have these wars been? Here is a list, from the longest to the shortest. (On-going: to mid-October, 2018, as this is written.)

Vietnam War	Nov, 1955–April, 1973	17.4 years
War in Afghanistan	Oct 2001–Present	17 years (On–going)
Moro Rebellion	1899–1913	14 years
Northwest Indian War	1785–1795	10 years
Iraq War	April, 2003–Dec, 2011	8.9 years
American Revolutionary War	April, 1775–Sept, 1783	8.5 years
Second Seminole War	Dec, 1835–Aug, 1842	6.7 years
War on ISIS	June, 2014–present	4.4 years
First Barbary War	May, 1801–June, 1805	4.1 years
American Civil War	April, 1861–April, 1865	4 years
World War II	Dec., 1941–Aug, 1945	3.8 years
Korean War	June, 1950–Aug, 1953	3.1 years
War of 1812	June, 1812–Dec, 1814	2.6 years
Red Cloud's War	July, 1866–April, 1868	1.9 years
Mexican-American War	April, 1846–Feb, 1848	1.9 years
World War I	April, 1917–Nov, 1918	1.7 years
Russian Civil War	Sept, 1918–April, 1920	I.7 years
Great Sioux War of 1876	Feb, 1878–May, 1877	1.3 years

Libya Civil War	March, 2011–Oct, 2011	7 months
Persian Gulf War	Aug, 1990–Feb, 1991	7 months
Whiskey Rebellion	May, 1794–Oct, 1794	5 months
Spanish-American War	April, 1898–August, 1898	114 days
Kosovo War	March, 1999–June, 1999	79 days
Invasion of Panama	Dec. 1989–Jan, 1990	42 days
Invasion of Grenada	Oct, 1983–Oct, 1983	4 days

There are those on the left and far-left and those on the right and far-right in the United States—and countless many in between—who would believe there were certainly wars worth fighting for: the American Revolution, to establish our Republic; the Civil War to maintain the Union; and the Second World War, which many believe was "the last good war."

Yet ... and yet ... since the advent of the twenty-first century, the United States has found itself increasingly bogged down in a series of endless wars .

Dan Simpson contributed this column to the *Pittsburgh Post-Gazette* May 18, 2011. And though it may appear to be slightly dated, from the perspective of the publication date, his observations are, as they say, spot on. (Simpson is a former U.S. ambassador and a *Post-Gazette* associate editor.)

Why can't we stop our wars?

There's no reason for the U.S.
to still be fighting in Iraq,
Afghanistan or Libya

America's wars tend to become tar babies. We put our hands into an overseas situation, they become gooey, stuck in complexity; then we can't bear to extract ourselves from the grimy mess.

One unfortunate and expensive aspect of this phenomenon is that we don't seem able to bring our forces home after a war is over.

World War II ended in 1945. The United States still has 52,000 troops in Germany, 49,000 in Japan and 10,000 in Italy, 66 years later. All sorts of imaginative arguments are put forward to support their continued presence—to provide regional security, to deter common enemies, to act as a tripwire, whatever. But Johnny doesn't come marching home.

Nor have forces left South Korea. That war ended in 1953. There are still 28,500 U.S. troops stationed there.

One place we didn't leave troops was Vietnam—because we lost.

Now we are enmeshed in Iraq, Afghanistan and Libya, where the war began in 2003, has 48,000 American troops. Afghanistan, which started in 2001, has 100,000. We don't know how many U.S. forces are now in Libya because our government hasn't chosen to tell us, or even call it a war. This avoids involving Congress and an examination of its rationale that observing legal procedures, notably the War Powers Act, would oblige.

So, instead of clean withdrawals to bring U.S. wars to an end, Americans are forced to watch and pay for endless, expensive occupations. Long, drawn-out screeches might come from taxpayers if they understood what was going on, but successive Republican and Democratic administrations pay no attention to call for peace dividends.

In 2008 President George W. Bush negotiated and signed with the Iraq government a status-of-forces agreement that provided for *all* U.S forces to be out of Iraq by Dec. 31, 2011. As the date draws high, some Iraqis—specifically those whom the United States was instrumental in putting in power and who thus have a stake in the status quo—are suggesting that maybe all U.S forces *shouldn't* leave by Dec. 31. They cite internal security, hostile neighbors and the like. There also is the delicate question of the United States continuing to pour money into Iraq after American troops leave.

It is fully predictable that Iraqis with an interest in U.S. forces staying would begin to say how nice it would be if they did. What is not acceptable is that some senior U.S. military and political figures, starting with Adm. Mike Mullen, chairman of the Joint Chiefs of Staff, are telling the Iraqis publicly that we would be glad to stay if they would just ask.

Such pleas and offers do not reflect the point of view of most Americans, who are ready to wind up that frustrating, expensive, eight-year-old war. The Iraq war may still be beloved of defense industry contractors, congressmen and senators who take their campaign donations and four-star military officers, but the average American is very tired of spending money and losing lives in Iraq.

The truly ironic aspect of the stay-or-leave Iraq debate is that we will probably be *forced* to leave because the occupation government of Prime Minister Nouri al-Mahiki is afraid to negotiate an extension of U.S. forces because of the unbending opposition of anti-American fellow Shitte Moktada al-Sadr. So we will be able to do what we should do for good *American* reasons—leave—thought the obdurate opposition to our staying of our most openly bitter enemy in Iraq.

It probably isn't necessary to use much space indicate why most Americans believe we should withdraw our 100,000 troops from Afghanistan, beginning in July as President Barack Obama promised. Al-Quida there is greatly reduced; its leader Osama bin Ladan, is dead; Pakistan as a base for the American war in Afghanistan is "bust" and most Afghans are ready to cut a deal with the Taliban, for at least part of the country to achieve peace after 10 years of destruction, mayhem and danger.

There again, pitted on the other side of a "clean withdrawl," are U.S. defense contractors,U.S. generals, the national security industry crowd and the thousands of Afghans on the U.S. pay-roll. The U.S. presence in Afghanistan costs at least $100 billion year.

Libya, a newer war, and Mr. Obama's very own undeclared, incomprehensible conflict, is also already stringing on long past its "sell-by" date. Secretary of Defense Robert M. Gates has help-fully told us that it has cost about $750 million to date. He can foresee no end to it. (Where have we heard that before?)

This war is allegedly justified why the need to protect Libyan civilians. (That's why NATO killed three of Libyan leader Moammar Gadhafi's grandchildren.) It is supposed to illustrate NATO's relevance and coherence. (Three countries and the United States out of 28 NATO members are engaged in Libya.)

Now, the still-divided, undisciplined, militarily incompetent rebel Libyans, unable even with heavy NATO air and ground support to gain much ground, are busily engaged in what such operations tend to evolve into. They are asking for big money.

They robbed the Gadhafi government's central bank of $200 million, but claim they need $30 billion from international do-nors, plus Libya's frozen assets. (How else are the rebellions's leaders to build up their offshore bank accounts for when it is time to bail out?)

In Benghazi, their "capital," night-roaming death sguads are murdering former Gadhafi officials. (This is supposedly bring done in the name of the justice they plan to bring to the place once NATO has put them in power.)

Again, why are we doing this in Libya? And continuing to try and run Iraq and Afghanistan?

The sharp budget debts in Washington are making it clear to Americans where our national priorities should be. They certainly do not lie in Baghdad, Kabul, Tripoli or Benghazi.

And Thomas E. Ricks writes:

In the post 9/11 era, *1984* particularly has found a new relevance, and a new generation readers ...

For present-day Americans, *1984*'s background of permanent warfare carries a chilling warning. In the book, as in American life today, the conflict is offstage, heard only as an occasional rocket impacts in the distance.

In an era when American wars are waged with drones firing precision-guided missiles, and with small numbers of Navy SEALS and other Special Operators Forces on the ground in remote parts of the Middle East, with occasional enemy bombings in cities such as London, Paris, Madrid and New York, this passage from the novel {*1984*) is eerily prescient:

It is a warfare of limited aims between combatants who are unable to destroy one another, (and) have no material cause for fighting ... (it) involves very small numbers of people, mostly highly trained specialists, and causes comparatively few casualties. The fighting, when there is any, takes place on vague frontiers whose whereabouts the average man can only guess at. In the centers of civilization war means no more than ... the occasional crash of a rocket bomb which may cause a few scores of deaths.

4

Constant surveillance

Behind Winston's back the voice from the telescreen
was still babbling away about pig-iron and the
overfulfillment of the Ninth Three-Year Plan.
The telescreen received and transmitted simultaneously.
—*1984*

Surveillance capabilities in America are now as much a permanent part of America as wars have been in the past—and present; and, if anything, surveillance, in all its aspects, is likely to grow larger, more complex and more secretive in the coming years.

In their report "Bigger Monster, Weaker Chains," for the American Civil Liberties Union, Jay Stanley and Barry Steinhardt write: "For decades, the notion of a 'surveillance society,' where every facet of our private lives is monitored and recorded, has sounded abstract, paranoid, or far-fetched to many people."

1984 also sounded abstract, paranoid or far-fetched too—in 1949.

(Orwell learned about the early advent of television and, during World War Two, he learned that an average telephone could be bugged so that when it wasn't in normal use, it also could be a listening device. His *telescreen* concept was a unique leap in Orwell's imagination and contributed significantly to *1984.*)

Background

Mass surveillance in the United States can be traced back to the early 20th century, when all international mail sent through the U.S. Postal Service and international cables sent through companies such as Western Union, ITT and RCA were sent under the surveillance authority of the Bureau of Investigation, later renamed the Federal Bureau of Investigation and reviewed by the U.S. military.

After World War 1, the U.S. Army and State Department established the Black Chamber, also known as the Cipher Bureau, which began operations in 1919. The Black Chamber was headed by Herbert 0. Yardley, who had been a leader in the Army's Military Intelligence program. Regarded as a precursor to the National Security Agency, it concluded peacetime decryption of material including diplomatic communications until 1919.

In the advent of World War 11, the Office of Censorship was established. The wartime agency monitored "communications by mail, cable, radio or, other means of transmission passing between the United States and any foreign country." This included the 350,000 overseas cables and telegrams and 25,000 international telephone calls made each week …. Every letter that crossed international or U.S. territorial borders from December 1941 to August 1945 was subject to being opened and scoured for details.

With the end of World War 11, Project SHAMROCK was established in 1945. The organization was created to accumulate telegraphic data entering and exiting from the United States. Major communications companies such as Western Union, RCA Global and ITT World Communications actively aided the project, allowing American intelligence officials to gain access to international message traffic. Under the project, and many subsequent programs, no precedent had been established for judicial authorization, and no warrants were issued for surveillance activities- The project was terminated in 1975.

In 1952, President Harry S. Truman established the National Security Agency (NSA) in 1952 for the purposes of collecting, processing and monitoring intelligence data. The existence of NSA was not known to people as the memorandum by President Truman was classified.

When the Citizen's Commission to Investigate the FBI published stolen FBI documents revealing abuse of intelligence programs in 1971, Senator Frank Church began an investigation into the programs that became known the Church Committee. The committee sought to investigate intelligence abuses throughout the 1970s. Following a report provided by the committee outlining egregious abuse, in 1976 Congress established the Senate Select Committee on Intelligence. It would later be joined by the Foreign Intelligence Surveillance Court in 1978. The institutions worked to limit the power of the agencies, ensuring that surveillance activity remained within the law.

Following the attacks of September 11, 2001, Congress passed the Patriot Act to strengthen security and intelligence efforts. The act granted the President broad powers on the war against terror including the power to bypass the FISA Court for surveillance orders in cases of national security. Additionally, mass surveillance activities were concluded alongside various other surveillance programs under the head of (the) President's Surveillance Program. Under pressure from the public, the warrantless wiretapping program was allegedly ended in January, 2007.

Many details about the surveillance activities conducted in the United States were revealed in the disclosure by Edward Snowden in June 2013.

Regarded as one of the biggest media leaks in the United States, it presented extensive details about the surveillance programs of the NSA, that involved interception of internet data and telephone calls from *over a billion users,* across various countries, (italics added.)

National Security Agency (NSA)

1947: The National Security Act was signed by President Harry S. Truman, establishing a National Security Council.

1949: The Armed Forces Security Agency was established to coordinate signal operations between military branches.

1952: The National Security Agency (NSA) was officially established by President Truman by way of a National Security Council Intelligence Directive 9, dated Oct. 24, while the NSA officially came into existence days later on Nov. 4. according to *The New York Times,* the NSA was created in "absolute secrecy" by President Truman, whose surveillance-minded administration ordered, only six weeks after President Truman took office, wiretaps on the telephones of Thomas Gardiner Corcoran, a close advisor of Franklin D. Roosevelt. The recorded conversations are currently kept at the Harry S. Truman Presidential Library and Museum, along with documents considered sensitive.

The FBI

The government agency that has been the most problematic over the years and decades has not been the National Security Agency (NSA) but the FBI, notably under the tenure of J. Edgar Hoover.

There have been a variety of books published over the years about Hoover and the FBI. One of the most revealing—and disturbing—has been Herbert Mitgang's *Dangerous Dossiers* (1988).

He writes:

> Early in this century, the United States Supreme Court was called upon to decide a case that foreshadowed dire events: domestic surveillance of citizens, political espionage of dissidents, unauthorized wiretapping and electronic eavesdropping, information banks and the panoply of offenses summed up in the words *Watergate*.
>
> In testimony before the Senate Judiciary Committee, Professor Arthur W.R. Miller of the Michigan and Harvard law schools once spoke darkly of a time of approaching "dossier dictatorship."
>
> The two concepts—privacy and dossiers—inevitably collide.
>
> The purpose of this book is to demonstrate by example that, in most cases, government dossiers are constitutionally unsound, fruitless and dangerous—dangerous not only to the individual who is harmed by having an unnecessary government record that follows him, and possibly his family, forever, but also to the nation's values and traditions of personal independence. Dossiers are a heritage of hysteria about radicalism and of the cold war. In the last decade much of the FBI's Hooverian paranoia has evaporated, thanks to congressional oversight and increased public awareness of the dangers of secret sub-governments. Nevertheless, in more recent times, lawlessness has been revealed on other, more radical levels that recall Sinclair Lewis's warning novel, *It Can't Happen Here*. The Iran-Contra hearings showed an interlocking network of official spies, mercenaries, former generals, opportunists and cold war profiteers

operating within government precincts but outside the Constitution and institutions of government.

Regarding government files—secret dossiers Mitgang also writes:

> ... during Hoover's reign—when most of the files were built up—the bureau was criticized for its excesses, rivalries with other agencies, political intrusion and actual violation of the laws that led to the exposure of its illegal extracurricular activities on the political front to suppress dissent. What has been undeniable—according to the memoirs of some of his own former colleagues in the bureau—is that the FBI was shaped in the image of one individual, J. Edgar Hoover. He was recognized as a fanatic on the subject of radicals, Communists, leftists and liberals, drawing hardly any distinction among them. As the files secured for this book indicate, many authors were categorized as internal security risks and branded Communists.
>
> Hoover was also racist, as evidenced by his voyeuristic pursuit of Martin Luther King Jr., lack of any significant number of blacks in the bureau, and outright stalling before he was forced to help the Justice Department handle civil rights cases in the South. He was a politician without portfolio who kept private files on public officials to blackmail them.

As Mitgang indicated, for years—indeed, for decades—Hoover seemed to conduct a personal holy war—a *jihad*—against famous writers, and many others in public life.

Mitgang used the Freedom of Information Act to obtain formerly secret files on the following, a veritable who's-who of international arts and letters and entertainment.

Among those the FBI had secret files on were:

Sinclair Lewis ... Pearl S. Buck ... William Faulkner ... Ernest Hemingway ... John Steinbeck ... Thomas Mann ... Carl Sandburg ... Theodore Dreiser ... John Dos Passos ... Thomas Wolfe ... Dorothy Parker ... John O'Hara ... Nelson Algren ... Dashiell Hammett ... Irwin Shaw ... Truman Capote ... A.J. Liebling ... Thornton Wilder ... Robert Sherwood ... Elmer Rice ... Maxwell Anderson ... Georgia O'Keeffe ... Tennessee Williams ... Frank Sinatra ... Martin Luther King, Jr. ... Norman Mailer ... John Kenneth Galbraith ... the Beatles ... John Lennon (separate file) ... Allen Ginsberg ... Eleanor Roosevelt ... Marilyn Monroe ... Walt Disney ... Albert Einstein ... E.B. White ... George Orwell ... and many others.

How did these individuals handle the possibility—or did they ever suspect—that they were under surveillance?

Here are two examples:

When John Steinbeck, a native of Salinas, California, published *The Grapes of Wrath,* in 1939, it became the epic moral vision of the 1930s.

It is commonly considered his greatest work. According to *The New York Times,* it was the bestselling book of 1939 and 430,000 copies had been printed by February, 1942. Later that year, it won the Pulitzer Price for fiction. California banks and large- scale growers were outraged at his picture of them in the novel.

Grapes was controversial. Steinbeck's New Deal political views, negative portrayal of aspects of capitalism, and sympathy for the plight of workers led to a backlash against him, especially close to home. Claiming the book was both obscene and misrepresented conditions in the county, The Kern County (California) Board of Supervisors banned the book from the county's publicly funded schools and libraries in August 1939. The ban lasted until January, 1941.

Steinbeck's reputation among some was that he was a Communist or Communist-sympathizer. (It didn't help that Steinbeck's first wife once registered to vote in California as a Communist just to see what would happen.)

He said, "The vilification of me out here from the large land-owners and bankers is pretty bad. The latest is a rumor stated by them that the Okies hate me and have threatened to kill me lying about them. I'm frightened at the rolling might of this damned thing. It is completely out of hand; I mean a kind of hysteria about the book is growing and it is not healthy."

Active surveillance apparently began post-1939.

By 1942 Steinbeck knew, but could not prove, that he was under surveillance and/or possibly being followed.

He wrote a postcard to then-Attorney General Francis Biddle:

Dear Mr. Biddle:
    … Do you suppose you could ask Edgar's boys to stop stepping on my heels? They think I am an enemy alien. It's getting tiresome …

The FBI, which had no sense of humor then or now, never forgave nor forgot Steinbeck's jab at "Edgar's boys."

During World War Two, federal investigators probed Steinbeck's personality and history to determine if he would be suitable to become an officer in the armed forces. One California government agent stated that Steinbeck was a patriotic American and *was* of sufficient moral character to be an officer, especially if his writing talents could be utilized by the military.

That recommendation was rejected; Steinbeck never served in the military during World War Two.

He did, instead, publish The *Moon is Down*, a novel; a thinly disguised portrait of Norway under the Nazis and *Bombs Away: The Story of a Bomber Team,* both in 1942. He donated the royalties from *Bombs Away* to Army Air Force charities.

There is some substantial argument that the publication of these two books was more of a contribution to the war effort than anything he could have done as an officer. (The Nazis considered that owning *The Moon is Down* was a death sentence to anyone in Scandinavia during World War Two.)

Surveillance did not stop; it continued and continued, throughout his lifetime. Steinbeck died in December, 1968, and the file apparently still continued *after his death*. Steinbeck's 1942 postcard jab at "Edgar's boys" was kept in Steinbeck's FBI file, literally for decades. After his death, his widow Elaine once said, "John would have roared with laughter if he had known (J. Edgar) Hoover might have been a homosexual or a crossdresser or both." (A common rumor then and perhaps still now.)

Ernest Hemingway lived on an estate outside Havana, Cuba, for twenty years—1940-1960. He owned a Cadillac, had a swimming pool and a motor yacht and lived like a king compared to the average Cuban during those days.

During the war years he conceived the idea of using his yacht, the Pilar, to hunt Nazi submarines in the waters outside Cuba. He convinced the American Ambassador in Cuba, Spruille Braden, to finance a crew and armaments for his sub-hunting. It was an outlandish idea at best; he believed he could conquer a Nazi submarine on the surface by dropping a hand grenade down the (open) conning tower.

The FBI under J. Edgar Hoover was outraged about this; and even more outraged that Spruille Braden not only approved of this idea, but gave Hemingway funds to do it.

The legal attache, i.e., an FBI man assigned to the Embassy in Havana, Raymond Leddy, sent regular reports about Hemingway to Hoover; one reply from Hoover to Leddy stated, "Hemingway's judgment is not of the best and if his sobriety is the same as it was some years ago, that is certainly guestionable." (Discrediting perceived foes of the FBI with comments such as those was a common FBI tactic under Hoover.)

Mitgang relates this anecdote about Hemingway:

> During the last twenty years of his life, Hemingway suspected he was a target of the FBI. His longtime lawyer, Alfred Rice, recently told me. "Whenever Ernest and I were at the Floridita in Cuba, he would sit at the end of the bar, protecting his back. Once he said to me, "You see those guys over there? They're agents, keeping an eye on me." It sounded a little strange at the time, but you know something? He may have been right."

Hemingway left Cuba in 1960, about the time of the advent of the Fidel Castro regime; Castro promised to keep his estate well maintained as a cultural/ historical site, as Hemingway was beloved by the Cuban people, but it fell into disrepair and neglect. His beloved yacht, the Pilar, in drydock, rotted away.

He moved to Ketchum, Idaho, for the hunting and mountains; Ketchum is also the location of the Sun Valley Ski Resort. Back in the United States, the FBI apparently decided that it was well within its purview to begin active surveillance. As he told A.E. Hotchner, a long-time friend:

> "It's the worst hell. The goddamnedest hell. They've bugged everything. THat's why we're using Duke's car. Mine's bugged. Everything's bugged. Can't use the phone. Mail intercepted. What put me on to it was that phone call with you. You remember we got disconnected? That tipped their hand."

Hemingway's health spiraled down and deteriorated into what one doctor described as "depressive/ persecutory." Doctors recommended treatment—first at Menninger's (hospital) but later decided on the Mayo Clinic, in Rochester, Minnesota. Because of (his) perceived obsession with the FBI, it was decided that he be admitted for a specific other reason, in his case, high blood pressure. He entered the Mayo Clinic in January, 1961. His condition seemed to improve and he was released the same month.

By April 23rd, Hemingway was in the Sun Valley Hospital under heavy sedation, given sodium amytal every three hours and nurses around the clock. His wife Mary had found him holding a shotgun in one hand with two shells his other hand; he had written a note to her. He read part of it—it was clearly a last note. She called a Hemingway friend, a local doctor, whom Hotchner called Vernon Lord, (in his memoir *Papa Hemingway)* who came. Hemingway gave him the shotgun. They agreed that Hemingway would need to go back to the Mayo Clinic.

Before he left, there was another *contretemps: as* a team arrived to pick up Hemingway to drive to a waiting charter plane, they found him again with a shotgun; he was ramming a shell into the chamber. They had to fight to get it away from him.

He had been given sedation before taking off, but in the air he tried to open the aircraft door and jump out; he had to be given another shot to keep him sedated for the rest of the flight.

The flight to the Mayo Clinic had to be delayed; they landed in Casper, Wyoming, for minor aircraft repairs. While there Hemingway tried to commit suicide by walking into the whirling propeller blades of another aircraft on the tarmac. A friend, Don Anderson, pulled him away but Anderson himself was nearly hit by the still whirling propellor.

He was back in the Mayo Clinic: it had no adjoining hospital; he was in nearby St. Mary's hospital, which had admitting agreements with the Mayo Clinic, just three months after he was first released—not a very long cure from the first treatment, Hotchner ruefully thought.

During his first stint at the Mayo Clinic, Hemingway was given 11 ECT treatments (Electro Convulsive Treatments). And more during his second stay at the Mayo Clinic. They were horrific, barbaric, a medieval treatment for the twentieth century; perhaps a unconscionable choice by his doctors. (Later, his widow Mary Hemingway considered suing the Mayo Clinic for medical malpractice, but ultimately decided not to.)

And, essentially, the ECT treatments *obliterated his memory.*

A writer has only two key elements in his or her arsenal: the memory of, and use of, writing techniques learned over decades, or perhaps a lifetime; and the memories—and perhaps writing about—past loves, experiences, marriage or marriages, friends, events, failures, achievements. His memoir of his much earlier Paris life and first marriage, *A Moveable Feast,* was published posthumously, in 1964; he had trouble working on it prior to, and during, his Mayo Clinic sessions.

The searing, horrific, treatments left him *a man without a soul, a haunted shell.*

Back in Ketchum, Ernest Hemingway took out his favorite shotgun, and committed suicide, July 1,1961.

There is no possible calculus of how much damage the years of FBI surveillance took on him; he was essentially right about it—all of it.

He once wrote:

> There are some things which cannot be learned quickly, and time, which is all we have, must be paid heavily for their acquiring. They are the very simplest

things, and because it takes a man's life to know them the little new that each man gets from life is very costly and the only heritage he has to leave.

—from Death in the Afternoon, 1932

Ernest Hemingway's heritage to the world was very large—and enduring.

How large were other FBI files? They were not trivial:

- John Lennon, 300 pages;
- Frank Sinatra: 1,300 pages;
- Albert Einstein, 1,500 pages;
- Eleanor Roosevelt: 3,000 pages;
- Martin Luther King, Jr., 17,000 pages.

There is no public record of any remorse by J. Edgar Hoover about the lives damaged or ruined by the needless FBI surveillances and, in truth, probably no private remorse from him either. None of these individuals surveilled by the FBI for years or decades was a threat to the safety of our American democracy. Ever. The Hoover years as head of the FBI were shameful in this regard; but today his name is on the FBI building in Washington, D.C., and likely to remain there.

Big Brother Is Watching You

The final report of the Church Committee revealed:

- Over 26, 000 individuals were at one point catalogued on an FBI list of persons to be rounded up in the event of a "national emergency";
- Over 500,000 domestic intelligence files were kept at FBI headquarters, of which 65,000 were opened in 1972 alone;

- At least 130,000 first class letters were opened and photographed by the FBI from 1940 to 1966;
- 250,000 first class letters were opened and photographed by the CIA from 1953 to 1973;
- Millions of private telegrams sent from, to, and through the United States were obtained by the National Security Agency (NSA) under a secret agreement with the U.S. telegraph companies, from 1947 to 1975;
- Over 100,000 Americans have bene indexed in U.S. Army intelligence files;
- About 300,000 individuals were indexed in a CIA computer system during the course of Operation CHAOS;
- Intelligence files on more than 11,000 individuals and groups were created by the Internal Revenue Service (IRS), with tax investigations "done on the basis of political rather than tax criteria."

Additionally, under the Mail Isolation Control and Tracking program the U.S. Postal Service-

photographed the exterior of every piece of paper mail processed in the United States—about 160 billion pieces in 2012. (italics added.)

The U.S. Postmaster General stated that the system is primarily used for mail sorting, but the images are available for possible use by law enforcement agencies.

And … billions of dollars per year are spent, by agencies such as the Information Awareness Office, National Security Agency (NSA) and the FBI to develop, purchase, implement and operate systems such as Carnivore, ECHELON, and NarusInsight to intercept and analyze the immense amount of data that traverses the internet and telephone systems each day.

And … The FBI developed the computer programs "Magic Lantern" and CIPAV, which it can remotely install on a computer system, in order to monitor a person's computer activity.

And … since the September 11, 2001 terrorist attacks, a vast domestic intelligence apparatus has been built to collect information using FBI, local police, state homeland security offices and military criminal investigators. The intelligence apparatus collects, analyzes and stores information about millions of (if not all) American citizens, most of whom have not been accused of any wrongdoing. Every state and local law enforcement agency is to feed information to federal authorities to support the work of the FBI.

And … law enforcement and intelligence services in the United States possess technology to remotely activate the microphone in cell phones in order to listen to conversations that take place nearby the person who holds the phone.

U.S. Federal agents regularly use mobile phones to collect location data. The geographical location of a mobile phone (and thus the person carrying it) can be determined easily, (whether it is being used or not), using a technigue known as multilateration to calculate the difference in time for a signal to travel from the cell phone to each of several cell towers near the owner of the phone.

And … Wide Area Persistent Surveillance (Also: Wide Area Motion Imaging) is a form of airborne surveillance system that collects pattern-of-life data by recording motion images of an area larger than a city—in sub-meter resolution. This video allows for anyone within the field of regard to be tracked—both live and retroactively, for forensic analysis … WAMI is currently in use on the southern border of the USA … the WAMI cameras … create airborne video so detailed that pedestrians can be followed across the city through forensic analysis. This allows investigators to rewind and playback the movements of anyone within this 68 square mile area for hours, days or even months at time …

And … traffic cameras, which were meant help enforce traffic laws at intersections, have also sparked some controversy, due to their use by law enforcement agencies for purposes unrelated to traffic violations. These cameras also work as transit chokepoints that allow individuals inside the vehicle to be positively identified and license plate data to be collected and time-stamped for cross reference with airborne WAMI systems.

And … On June 19, 2013, FBI Director Robert Mueller told the United States Senate Committee on the Judiciary that the federal government had been employing surveillance drones on U.S. soil in "particular incidents." According to Mueller, the FBI is currently in the initial stage of developing drone policies.

Earlier in 2012, Congress passed a US $63 billion bill that will grant four years of additional funding to the Federal Aviation Administration (FAA) . Under the bill, the FAA is required to provide military and commercial drones with expended access to U.S. airspace by October, 2015.

In February 2013, a spokesman for the Los Angeles Police department explained that these drones would initially be deployed in large public gatherings, including major protests. Over time, tiny drones would be used to fly inside buildings to track down suspects and assist in investigations. According to *The Los Angeles Times,* the main advantage of using drones is that they offer "unblinking eye-in-the-sky coverage."

They can be modified to carry high-resolution video cameras, infrared sensors, license plate readers, listening devices and be disguised as sea gulls or other birds to mask themselves.

By 2020, about 30,000 unmanned drones are expected to be deployed in the United States for the purpose of surveillance and law enforcement.

(And surely there are other, newer, even more sophisticated surveillance systems in place now, still ultra secret.)

We have all heard—and used—this old canard:

There are only two true things, death and taxes.

Now, the canard should be up-dated:

In the United States, there are four true things:
death, taxes, never-ending wars
and constant surveillance.

5

Prohibited Sex

When Winston and Julia wanted to find somewhere private to be lovers, as sex was prohibited by Big Brother, they had to find a dingy room without a telescreen or venture into the country outside London, so they could not only be away from the telescreens but also away from the Thought Police …

… in America, the fight for, (and against), sexual mores continues—in another area. This fight can be summarized in one landmark legal case: Roe versus Wade, commonly called Roe vee Wade.

Roe v. Wade is now a landmark case, issued by the Supreme Court in 1973, which decided the constitutionally of laws that criminalized or restricted access to abortions. The court ruled 7-2 that a right to privacy under the Due Process Clause of the 14th Amendment extended to a women's decision have an abortion, but that right must be balanced against the state's interests in regulating abortions: protecting women's health and protecting the potentially of human life.

This was a delicate legal balancing test—how to resolve it? The court tied state regulation of abortion to the third trimester of pregnancy.

The key was *fetal viability*: that the fetus would be "potentially able to live outside the mother's womb, albeit with artificial aid." The Roe case acknowledged that viability may occur at 23 or 24 weeks into the pregnancy, sometimes earlier, in light of medical advancements.

Since 1973, the Roe case has sparked continued debate about whether, and to what extent, abortions should be legal in the United States; who should decide the legality of abortion; what methods the Supreme Court should use and what the contributions of religious groups and moral views should be.

Roe has reshaped national politics, dividing much of the population of the United States into *pro-life* and *pro-choice* divisions, while generating vast grassroots movements on both sides.

The background of the case is now straightforward history: In June, 1969, Texas resident Norma McCorvey, then 21, discovered she was pregnant with her third child. Friends urged her to get an abortion under the (false) claim that she had been raped; that scheme failed when there was no police report of a rape. She then attempted to get an illegal abortion, but found the unauthorized facility had been closed by the local police. She was eventually referred to attorneys Linda Coffee and Sarah Weddington.

(McCorvey gave birth before the case was resolved and the child was given up for adoption.)

The then-Texas law stated that abortion was permissible only to save the life of the mother.

Coffee and Weddington filed suit in the United States District Court for the Northern District of Texas, on behalf of McCorvey, under the alias Jane Roe. Defending the State of Texas was Dallas County District Attorney Henry Wade.

On June 17, 1970 a three-judge panel, consisting of Sarah T. Hughes, William McLaughlin Taylor Jr. and Irving Loeb Goldberg, unanimously declared the Texas law unconstitutional, finding it violated the right of privacy found in the Ninth Amendment.

The case reached the Supreme Court in 1970, on appeal. Sarah Weddington continued the case for McCorvey, i.e., Jane Roe.

(At that time there were *no* female Supreme Court justices.)

The Supreme Court issued its opinion January 22, 1973, with a 7-2 majority in favor of Roe.

The Court declined to adopt the district court's Ninth Amendment rationale, and instead asserted that the "right of privacy, whether it be founded in the Fourteenth Amendment's concept of personal liberty and restrictions upon state action, as we feel it is, or, as the district court determined, in the Ninth Amendment's reservation of rights to the people, is broad enough to encompass a woman's decision whether or not to terminate her pregnancy."

Justice Blackmun's majority opinion explicitly rejected a fetal "right to life" argument. The Court instead recognized the right to an abortion as a fundamental right included within the guarantee of personal privacy. As a result, regulations limiting abortion had to be justified by a "compelling state interest" and legislative enactments regulating abortion had to be narrowly tailored to meet the compelling interests; in other words, Justice Blackmun applied a strict analysis to abortion regulations.

While acknowledging that the right to abortion was not unlimited, Justice Blackmun, speaking for the Court, created a trimester framework to balance the fundamental right to abortion with the government's two legitimate interests: protecting the woman's health and protecting the "potentiality of human life." The trimester framework addressed when a women's fundamental right to abortion would be absolute, and when the state's interest's would be compelling. In the first trimester, when it was believed that the procedure was safer than childbirth, the Court left the decision to abort complete to the woman and her physician.

From approximately the end of the first trimester until fetal viability, the state's interest in protecting the health of the mother would become "compelling." At that time, the estate could regulate the abortion procedure if the regulation "reasonably relate(d) to the preservation and protection of maternal health." At the point of viability, which the court believed would be in the third trimester, the state's interest in "potential life" would become compelling, and the state could regulate abortion to protect "potential life." At that point, the state could even forbid abortion so long as it made an exception to persevere the life or health of the mother.

The majority opinion allowed states to protect fetal life after viability even though a fetus is not a person within the meaning of the Fourteenth Amendment.

Writing on the website billmoyers.com, Irin Carmon summarized the perhaps surprising early history of abortion, then pre- and post-*Roe,* in the following essay. She is the co-author of *Notorious RBG: The Life and Times of Ruth Bader Ginsburg.*

A Brief History of Abortion Law in America

It's only become a hot-button issue in recent decades. For America's first century, abortion wasn't banned in a single U.S. state.

Abortion is as old as antiquity. As long as people have been having sex, there have been women having abortions. The American debate over whether a woman should have the right to end her pregnancy is a relatively new phenomenon. Indeed, for America's first century, abortion wasn't even banned in a single U.S. State.

Even the definition of abortion was different. In early America, as in Europe, "What we would now identify as an early induced abortion was not called an 'abortion' at all," writes Leslie Reagan in *When Abortion Was a Crime: Women, Medicine, and Law in the United States, 1867-1973.* "If an early pregnancy ended, it has 'slipp(ed) away,' or the menses had been 'restored.' At conception and the earliest stage of pregnancy, before quickening, no one believed that a human life existed; not even the Catholic Church took this view." Abortion was permissible until a women felt a fetus move, or "quicken." Back then, Reagan notes, "the popular ethic regarding abortion and common law were grounded in the female experience of their own bodies."

When US states did begin banning abortion in the 19th century, doctors seeking to drive out traditional healers, or in their words, quacks, often led the way. They had help from nativists who were concerned about women's growing independence and the country's growing diversity. Contemplating the colonization of the West and South in 1868, anti-abortion campaigner Dr. Horatio R. Storer asked if these frontiers would be "filled by our own children or by those of aliens? This is question our woman must answer; upon their loins depends the future destiny of the nation." Who would control those loins, and indeed whose childbearing is considered desirable, lay at the heart of regulations on abortion and contraception across the centuries.

The laws every state passed by 1880 banned abortions in all cases but for "therapeutic reasons." That were largely left up to the medical practice and the legal system to determine. In practice, that meant wealthier women with better access to doctors had abortions, while other women bled. "One stark indication of the prevalence of illegal abortion was the death toll," writes Rachel Benson Gold of the Guttmacher Institute. "In 1930, abortion was listed as the official cause of death for almost 12,700 women—nearly one-fifth (18 percent) of maternal deaths recorded in that year." Fatalities began decreasing with the advent of antibiotics to treat sepsis, but this too depended on one's status. "In New York City in the early 1960s," Benson Gold writes, "1 in 4 child-birth- related deaths among white women was due to abortion; in comparison, abortion accounted for 1 in 2 childbirth-related deaths among nonwhite and Puerto Rican women."

As other countries began liberalizing their abortion laws, women who could afford it began circulating pamphlets on how to make the trip. At least hundreds of women went to Mexico, England, Sweden—even Asia. The California-based Society for Humane Abortion, founded in 1961, explained how West Coast women could go as far as Japan to terminate: "If they want to know why you want to get the passport in hurry, tell them you are meeting a tour group in Japan and you didn't know you could go till just now ... Try to get the price reduced. Tell they you are a student or a poor working girl and don't have much money." The Chicago-based Jane, founded in the late 1960s, famously had a hotline where woman could ask for "Jane" to be referred to an illegal abortion, and eventually members began perform-ing abortions themselves. By 1973, these women had performed an estimated 11,000 abortions. "The women in the service were bold, and there was a growing women's movement which was about taking our lives into our own hands," recalled Jane co-founder Heather Booth.

Some feminists historically had been ambivalent about abor-tion. The move to repeal the abortion bans was initially driven by doctors appalled at the women with perforated uteruses lin-ing up at emergency rooms and a budding environmentalist movement worried about population growth. "Feminists sought to free women to participate fully and equally in the workplace, calling for contraception and abortion rights that would give women control over the timing of motherhood, at the same time that the movement sought public support for child care," writes

Linda Greenhouse and Reva Siegel in *Before Roe v. Wade: Voices That Shaped The Abortion Debate Before the Supreme Court's Ruling,* "only gradually, against the backdrop of the 1960s' understanding that sexual expression was a good independent of its procreative aims, did abortion rights migrate to the top of the women's rights agenda."

There were no paeans to sexual expression or women's freedom in *Roe v. Wade.* Nixon appointee Harry Blackmun wrote mostly about doctors' rights, ignoring arguments about women's equality but concluding that "the right of personal privacy includes the abortion decision, but that this right is not unqualified and must be considered against important state interests in regulation." The effect was sweeping: On a single day in 1973, all those 19th century bans were wiped out, and states could only ban abortion at fetal viability.

'Though history has nearly obscured it, Blackmun did not go out on a partisan limb. Five of the justices in the seven-justice majority in *Roe v. Wade,* were appointed by Republicans. As recently as 1972, a Gallup poll had found that a majority (64 percent) thought "the decision to have an abortion should one made solely by a woman and her physician." Republicans, at 68 percent, supported abortion rights most firmly of all.

The most recent Gallup data shows that exactly half of Americans say abortion should be "legal only under certain circumstances," while a third say it should be legal in all circumstances If you're keeping track, that means a minority—18 percent—want abortion banned entirely. And yet that view is represented by the president (who promised during the campaign to appoint justices who would overturn *Roe v Wade,* and has already appointed one likely Roe skeptic) and majorities in Congress and statehouses. Indeed, "since *Roe v. Wade,*" says Guttmacher analysis Elizabeth Nash, "there have been, 1,187 restrictions enacted at the state level."

These days, not only do anti-abortion activists want the procedure to be illegal at any stage of pregnancy, they even an to redefine common forms of birth control, like the intrauterine device, or IUD, and emergency contraception as abortion. This view has quickly reached the mainstream. In 2012, the Republican nominee for president declared "Contraception, it's working just fine. Leave it alone." Today, an opponent of contraception, Teresa Manning, heads the federal family planning program. Manning has said "family planning is what occurs between a husband, wife and God" and has opposed the use of contraceptives for years. America has come a long way since the days of "quickening."

What are the positions of the U.S. political parties on this issue?

- Though members of both major political parties come down on either side of this issue, the Republican Party is often seen as being pro-life, since the official party platform opposes abortion and considers unborn children to have an inherent right to life. Republicans for Choice represents the minority of that party. In 2006, pollsters found that 9 percent of Republicans favor the availability of abortion in most circumstances. Of Republican National Convention delegates in 2004, 13 percent believed that abortion should be generally available, and 38 percent believed that it should not be not permitted. The same poll showed that 17 percent of all Republican voters believed that it should be generally available to those who want it, while 38 percent believed that should not be permitted.
- The Democratic Party platform considers abortion to be a women's right. Democrats for Life of America represents the minority of that party. In 2006, pollsters

found that 74 percent of Democrats favor the availability of abortion in most circumstances. However, a Zogby International poll in 2004 found that 43 percent of all Democrats believed that abortion "destroys a human life, and is manslaughter." Of Democratic National Convention delegates in 2004, 75 percent believed that abortion should be generally available, and 2 percent believed that abortion should not be permitted. The same poll showed that 4 9 percent of all Democratic voters believed that abortion should be generally available to those who want it, and 13 percent believed it should not be permitted.

- The Green Party of the United States supports legal abortion as a women's right.
- The Libertarian Party platform states that "government should be kept out of the matter, leaving the guestion to each person for their conscientious consideration." Abortion is a contentious issue among Libertarians, and the Maryland-based organization Libertarians for Life opposes the legality of abortion in most circumstances.
- In the United States the debate has become deeply politicized: in 2002, 84 percent of state Democratic platforms supported the right to having an abortion, while 88 percent of Republican platforms opposed it. This divergence also led to Christian Right organizations such as Christian Voice, Christian Coalition and Moral Majority having an increasingly strong role in the Republican Party. This opposition has been extended under the Foreign Assistance Act: in 1973 Jesse Helms introduced an amendment banning the use of aid money to promote abortion overseas, and in 1984 the Mexico City Policy prohibited financial support to any overseas

organization that performed or promoted abortions. The "Mexico City Policy" was revoked by President Bill Clinton and subseguently reinstalled by President George W. Bush. President Barack Obama overruled this policy by Executive Order on January 23, 2009. And it was reinstalled on January 23, 2017 by President Donald Trump.

Although some of these statistics date back to 2002, the issue remains largely static: the Republican Party remains staunchly pro-life and the Democratic party remains just as staunchly pro-choice.

The abortion question—pro-life or pro-choice—is the ultimate cultural dividing issue of our time. It is not likely to ever be fully decided in your lifetime or mine.

And, as a coda to the Roe vee Wade lengthy legal case, Norma McCorvey, the original Jane Roe, eventually became a pro-life advocate. In 1998, she testified before Congress:

> "It was my pseudonym, Jane Roe, which had been used to create the 'right' to abortion out of legal thin air. But Sarah Weddington and Linda Coffee never told me that what I was signing would allow women to come up to me, 15, 20 years later and say, 'thank you for allowing me to have my five or six abortions. Without you it wouldn't have been possible.' Sarah never mentioned women using abortions as form of birth control. We talked about truly desperate and needy women, not women already wearing maternity clothes."

6

Black sites

Black sites: an Orwellian *1984* neologism?

It's circa 2006 American/CIA military slang for secret prisons for terrorists.

And: *extraordinary rendition* or *irregular rendition* or *forced rendition* (i.e., illegal) governmental- sponsored abduction and the extrajudicial transfer of a person—a terrorist or suspected terrorist—from one country, to another, carried out by the U.S. government, usually the C.I.A. These too, could easily be *1984* neologisms.

And like other governmental scandals, including Watergate, this one unraveled slowly:

- *The Washington Post* began coverage on December 26, 2002, reporting on a secret CIA prison in one corner of the Bagram Air Force Base in Afghanistan;
- On March 14, 2004, the (British) *Guardian* newspaper reported that three British citizens were held captive in a secret section (Camp Echo) of the Guantanamo Bay complex in Cuba;
- The human rights organization, Human Rights Watch issued a report, "Enduring Freedom—Abuses by US Forces in Afghanistan, " stating that the CIA had oper-ated in Afghanistan since September 2001, maintaining

a large faculty in the Ariana Chowk neighborhood of Kabul and an interrogation and detention faculty at the Bagram Airbase;

- In the issues of February 26, to March 4, 2004 the Irish magazine *Village* reported "Abductions via Shannon," claimed that the Dublin and Shannon airports were used "by the CIA to abduct suspects in its 'war on terror.'" Flight logs from a Boeing 737, registered as N313P and later registered as N4476S showed it was routed through Shannon and Dublin with flights to: Estonia; Kabul; Skopje; Baghdad and later to Dubai; Baghdad again, and elsewhere. All flights ended in Washington, D.C. One flight landed in Guantanamo Bay having traveled from Poland, Romania and Morocco;

- The November 2, 2005 issue of *The Washington Post* carried an article that blew the story full-open.

  Reporter Dana Priest wrote, "The CIA has been hiding and interrogating some of its most important alleged al Qaeda captives at a Soviet-era compound in Eastern Europe, according to U.S. and foreign officials familiar with the arrangement." The article claimed that there was a network of foreign prisons including sites in several eastern European democracies, and Thailand, Afghanistan and a section of the Guantanamo Bay prison in Cuba. The network had been named the "Gulag Archipelago," in a clear reference to the novel of the same name by Russian novelist and activist Aleksandr Solzhenitsyn. The *Post* stated that the exact names of the eastern European countries were omitted at the request of Bush administration officials;

- A Human Rights Watch report dated November 3, 2005 confirmed the earlier *Village* articles that the Boeing 737 registered as N4476S was leased by the CIA to transport prisoners from Kabul, making stops in Poland and Romania, continuing to Morocco before flying to Guantanamo in Cuba. The article brought denials from the Polish and Romanian governments;

- An Amnesty International report dated November 8, 2005 provided the first comprehensive testimony from former inmates of the CIA black sites. The report documented the cases of three Yemeni nationals, who described conditions in the black site detention facilities in detail. A subsequent report by Amnesty International in April, 2006 used flight records to locate the base in eastern Europe.

- On September 6, 2006, President George Bush publicly admitted the existence of secret prisons and announced that many of the detainees held elsewhere were being transferred to Guantanamo Bay.

- Responding to the allegations about black sites, Secretary of State Condoleezza Rice stated, on December 5, 2005, that the U.S. had not violated any country's sovereignty in the rendition of suspects, and that individuals were never rendered to countries where it was believed that they night be tortured. Some in the media and other skeptics noted that her comments did not exclude the possibility of covert prison sites operated with the knowledge of the "host" nation, or that the promises by such "host" nations that detainees would not be tortured may not be genuine.

- *Washington Post* reporter Dana Priest subsequently won a Pulitzer Prize for her reporting about the CIA's black sites program.

- In a September 29, 2006 speech, George Bush stated, "Once captured, Abu Zubaydah, Ramzi bin al-Shibh and Khalid Sheikh Mohammed were taken into custody of the Central Intelligence Agency. The questioning of these and other suspected terrorists provided information that helped us protect the American people. They helped us break up a cell of Southwest Asian terrorist operatives that had been groomed for attacks inside the United States. They helped us disrupt an al Qaeda operation to develop anthrax for terrorist attacks. They helped us stop a planned strike on a U.S. Marine camp in Djibouti, and to prevent a planned attack on the U.S. Consulate in Karachi, and to foil a plot to hijack passenger planes and to fly them into Heathrow Airport and London's Canary Wharf."

- On July 20, 2007, President Bush issued an executive order banning torture of captives by intelligence officials.
- In a September 7, 2007, public address to the Council on Foreign Relations in New York, rare for a sitting Director of Central Intelligence, General Michael Hayden praised the program of detaining and interrogating prisoners, and credited it with providing 70 percent of the National Intelligence Estimate in the threat to America released in July. Hayden said the CIA had detained fewer than 100 people at secret facilities abroad since 2002, and even fewer prisoners have been secretly transferred to or from foreign governments. In a 20-minute question-and-answer session with the audience, Hayden disputed assertions that the CIA has used waterboarding, stress positions, hypothermia and dogs to interrogate suspects—all techniques that have been broadly criticized.

"That's a pretty good example of taking something to the darkest corner of the room and not reflective of what my agency does," Hayden told one person from a human rights organization.

In sum:

An estimated 50 prisons have been used to hold detainees in 28 countries, in addition to at least 25 more prisons in Afghanistan and 20 in Iraq. It is estimated that the U.S. has also used 17 ships as floating prisons since 2001, bringing the total estimated numbers of prisons operated by the U.S. and/ or its allies to house alleged terrorist suspects since 2001 to more than 100.

Big Brother would be proud.

7

Torture

"Do it to Julia—"
—Winston Smith, in *1984*

Then: *Rats!*

A primal fear of countless millions around the world—hungry rats, large rats—*huge rats*—nearby and getting closer …

In *1984,* Winston Smith and his love, Julia, are caught by the Thought Police in a dingy antiques shop; and are imprisoned in the Ministry of Love. Smith is interrogated by O'Brien, whom Smith knows; O'Brien is one step above him in The Party. Over months, Smith is forced to "cure" himself of his "insanity," by changing his beliefs to fit The Party line, even believing that 2+2=5, even though he knows that's not true.

O'Brien admits that The Party "is not interested in the good of others; it is interested solely in power."

Winston Smith is finally taken to Room 101; every prisoner's worst fears of The Party. As a wire cage of hungry rats is fitted over his head (his own worst fear realized), he shouts in abject panic, "Do it to Julia," thus betraying her. (She also betrays him in the same Room 101, in the same way.)

Where did Orwell get the concept of the hungry-rats—in-a-cage, Smith's worst fear (and indeed the fear of countless others)? For those who have read the Orwell canon, he mentions large rats in his quarters in *Homage to Catalonia,* during his stint with the P.O.U.M. in the Spanish Civil War.

But there is more to the backstory than that. William Steinhoff tells the story in his 1975 book, *George Orwell and the Origins of 1984.* (He mentions the G.P.U.: the State Political Administration, i.e., the Soviet Secret Service which existed until 1923, when it was renamed. *The Woman Who Could Not Die* was published in 1938.)

> … we must take notice of a book that was apparently in Orwell's library but which he seems not to have reviewed, Julia de Beausobre's *The Woman Who Could Not Die.* Mme de Beausobre and her husband were arrested in 1932 by the G.P.U. after having been banished to Samarkand for a year. M. De Beausobre was shot in 1933, and his wife Julia, was jailed in various Soviet prisons and prison camps for a long time before she was at last ransomed by English friends. When the book first appeared in 1938 it did not receive much notice, but after it was reissued in 1948 with an introduction by Rebecca West it secured a rather better reputation.
>
> The book is marked by the unquestionable authority with which the writer conveys the reality of what it means to be buried in a Soviet prison. She recounts all the details of life in solitary confinement—the silence, the vigilance of the guards, the painful naked light, the alternating cruelty and kindness. "Strange life!" she comments, "To be forced to the brink of madness, to be set in conditions that make you supremely vulnerable to any sort of illness and yet be solicitously doctored—twice a

day." Except for the "conveyor-belt" system of interrogations, the solitary cell life she endured for a long time
was dominated by dreams and fantasies. She testifies to
the great bond formed "between the man who is tortured day in, day out, and the man who day in, day out,
tortures him." She tried to protect herself, she says, by
deliberately forgetting as much as she could of the past,
because any mention of it could have been dangerous to
her or her husband; but, as she once cries out: "Can you
accept a long life with a mind entirely void of memory?
The divine gift of memory." Despite her physical and
mental suffering, Julia de Beausobre withstood the interrogations and was temporarily reprieved, but at last she
was called again and told "We only kill those of whom
we think very highly and those whom we despise pro-
foundly. You cannot doubt that we think highly of you."
To which she replied, "I shall console myself with that
when I am dying."

When such threats as this are ineffectual in making
her confess to things she had not done, the GPU transferred her to another prison and thence to Siberia, to
which she was sentenced for five years. In the new camp
she found that the inmates had careers and families. The
prison life engulfed her and them; it was not a hiatus; its
was a new "normal" life. But the rigors of this existence
nearly killed Julia, the rats were particular evil. In large
numbers they hurried boldly about the camp searching
for food, and Julia could not learn to lie quietly in bed
while a rat crawled over her.

> Rat! I realize, jumping to my feet and hurting
> them so that I sit down quickly on the bed next to
> mine. The woman in it ... cannot understand my

strange behaviour. The others who happen to be awake think me foolish, I suppose I am, why should I mind a rat after all? I must learn not to.

One cannot argue without more evidence that Orwell remembered this book when he wrote *1984*, but it touches *1984* at so many points, most notably on the side of the emotions, that the name "Julia"—if nothing more—would appear to survive from Orwell's recollections of Mme de Beausobre's moving narrative.

Now: *Waterboarding*

In George Orwell's fictional dystopian world circa 1948, the torture of choice was rats. In today's world, the choice has been waterboarding.

To be clear: Waterboarding is an International War Crime.

No matter that U.S. administration officials have called it an "enhanced interrogation technique" it is still an International War Crime.

Waterboarding—defined

Waterboarding is an enchanted interrogation technique that stimulates the feeling of being drowned. A person is strapped to a board with upper part of his body on a downward incline of 10 to 20 degrees. A cloth is placed over the person's mouth, and water is poured over his face, causing an almost immediate gag reflex and causing the person to have difficulty breathing and to feel as if his lungs are filling with water. CIA medical staff determined that the process is dangerous enough that they required resuscitation and medical equipment to be placed in interrogation rooms where waterboarding took place. On at least one occasion, a detainee required resuscitation.

Waterboarding—the history

Those who believe waterboarding is a modern interrogation torture technique need to re-read history: it goes back as far as the Spanish Inquisition in the 1500s. A book on the practice of criminal law, *Praxis rerum criminalium*, published in Antwerp, in 1554, has a chapter on waterboard and an accompanying woodcut showing the technique, remarkably similar to the techniques used today:

- Agents of the Dutch East India Company used the practice in 1623;
- An article in *The New York Times* April 6, 1852, detailed the use of a waterboard-type incident in the New York state prison Sing Sing. The practice was then called "showering" or "hydropathic torture";
- Prisoners in late-19th century Alabama and in Mississippi in the early 20th century also suffered waterboarding;
- The U.S. Army used waterboarding, then called the "water cure," during the Philippine-American War. Elihu Root, then U.S Secretary of War, ordered a court martial for one officer, Captain/Major Edwin F. Glenn, who eventually was fined fifty dollars and suspended. President Theodore Roosevelt ordered a court martial for General Jacob Smith, then serving on the island of Samar; when the court martial found that Smith had only "acted with excessive zeal," Roosevelt disregarded the verdict and had Smith dismissed from the Army;

- During World War Two, both the Japanese *Kempeitai* and the Nazi Gestapo used waterboarding, as torture;
- Chase J. Nielsen, one of the American airmen who served in the Doolittle raid was waterboarded by the Japanese after his capture;
- The French used waterboarding during the Algerian War (1954-1962). A French journalist, Henri Alleg, stated that the accidental death of prisoners subjected to waterboarding in Algeria was "very frequent";
- U.S. generals declared waterboarding an international war crime during the Vietnam war. But *The Washington Post* published a front-page article and photograph (January 21, 1968) showing two U.S. soldiers and one South Vietnam soldier waterboarding a North Vietnam POW. One U.S. soldier was court martialed by a U.S. military court within one month of the incident and he was dismissed from the Army;
- Northern Ireland used waterboarding in the 1970s;
- Post Vietnam, the Khmer Rouge used waterboarding between 1975 and 1979; Waterboarding, called "tubing" or the "wet bag technigue," was used by the South African Police during Apartheid.

Volunteering to be waterboarded

Christopher Hitchens, who published *Why Orwell Matters* and a variety of other books, volunteered to be waterboarded; his article "Believe Me, It's Torture" appeared in the August 2008 issue of *Vanity Fair* magazine. He was 59 at the time, well past the age of any appropriate volunteering and with a long history of cigarette smoking.

He contacted appropriate people (he did not specify who in his article) and journeyed to a rural area in North Carolina (Fort

Bragg or the Fort Bragg area, perhaps?); he signed an agreement that there would be safeguards provided "during the 'water boarding' process, however, these measures may fail and even if they work properly they may not prevent Hitchens from experiencing serious injury or death."

He had to produce a doctor's certificate stating that he did not have asthma.

He was eventually grabbed from behind and suddenly bound to a table; and he was reminded of *1984*:

> As a boy reading the climatic torture scene in 1984, where what is in Room 101 is the worst thing in the world, I realize that somewhere in my version of that hideous chamber comes the moment when the wave washed over me.

He later wrote:

> You many have read by now the official lie about this treatment, which is it "simulates" the feeling of drowning. This is not the case. You feel that you are drowning because you are drowning—or rather, being drowned, albeit slowly and under controlled conditions and at the mercy (or otherwise) of those who are applying the pressure.

He described the first experience—a slow cascade of water up his nose; he determined to resist, held his breath, then exhaled. Then attempted to inhale. And suddenly didn't know if he was exhaling or inhaling; he was flooded with panic and gave a pre-arranged sign to stop.

After a short period after being pulled upright, the routine began again. He fought again and discovered he was "an abject prisoner of my gag reflex":

> *The interrogators would hardly have any time to ask me any questions, and I knew that I would quite readily have agreed to supply any answer.*

And that, indeed, is the core problem of any torture and interrogation: the prisoner will say anything—*anything*—to make the torture stop, even though he knows the answers are untrue and self- serving .

Hitchens found himself clawing at the air with a horrible sensation of smothering. An interrogator, seeing this, said, "Any time is a long time when you're breathing water."

And, Hitchens thought:

> *I was hit with a ghastly sense of the sadomasochistic dimension that underlies the relationship between the torturer and the tortured.*

Just as Julia de Beausobre—and countless others—have experienced in prisons or captivity.

Hitchens was stunned to feel an index finger probing for his solar plexus. Why? He was later told:

> *That's to find out if you are trying to cheat, and timing your breathing to the (water) doses. If you try that, we can outsmart you. We have all kinds of enhancements.*

All kinds of enhancements. Clinical. Cold.

Hitchens quotes Malcolm Nance, whose most recent book (at that time) was *The Terrorists of Iraq.*

Nance offered these four guidelines for waterboarding:

1.   Waterboarding is a deliberate torture technigue and has been prosecuted as such by our judicial arm when perpetrated by others;
2.   If we allow it and justify it, we cannot complain if it is

employed in the future by other regimes on captive U.S. citizens. It is a method of putting American prisoners in harm's way;

3. It may be a means of extracting information, but it is also a means of extracting junk information;

4. It opens a door that cannot be closed. Once you have posed the notorious "ticking bomb" question, and once you assume that you are in the right, what will you *not* do? Waterboarding not getting results fast enough? The terrorist's clock still ticking? Well, then, bring on the thumbscrews and pincers and the electrodes and the rack.

Hitchens survived his trial with waterboarding, convinced beyond any doubt, that waterboarding is, indeed, torture.

(Hitchens died at 62, Dec. 16, 2011, in a Texas hospital from pneumonia, a complication of esophageal cancer.)

How waterboarding affects the body

Long-term damage to the human body by waterboarding can result in:

- Damages to muscles, arms, legs, as a result of thrashing in restraints;
- Permanent brain damage as a result of lack oxygen to the brain;
- Pneumonia from water in the lungs;
- Heart trouble, from heart muscle stress;
- Throat spasms;
- Damage to the intestines from ingesting excessive water;
- Long term psychological problems, including sleeplessness, the inability to sustain relationships with others, fears and phobias …

The C.I.A. waterboarded the wrong man 83 times in one month

The George W. Bush administration is now tied irrevocably with waterboarding—and torture:

In August 2002 and March 2003, in its war on terror, the George W. Bush administration, through Jay S. Bybee, the Office of Legal Counsel (OLC), Department of Justice, issued what became known as the Torture Memos after being leaked in 2004. These legal opinions (including a 2002 Bybee memo), argued for a narrow definition of torture under US law. The first three were addressed to the CIA, which took them as authority to use the described enhanced interrogation techniques (more generally known as torture) on detainees classified as enemy combatants. Five days before the March 2003 invasion of Iraq, John Yoo, the acting Office of Legal Counsel, issued a fouth memo to the General Counsel of DOD, concluding his legal option by saying that federal laws related to torture and other abuse did not apply to interrogations over-seas. The legal opinions were withdrawn by Jack Goldsmith of the OLC in June 2004 but reaffirmed by the succeeding head of the OLC in December, 2004. US government officials at various times said they did not believe waterboarding to be a form of torture.

In 2006, the Bush administration banned torture including waterboarding on detainees, but only for the US Military, not the CIA. When an amendment by Senator Dianne Feinstein passed that restricted use on the CIA, President Bush vetoed the bill. In January, 2009, U.S President Barack Obama issued a similar ban on the use of waterboarding and other forms of torture in interrogations on detainees. In April 2009, the U.S. Department of Defense refused to say whether waterboarding is still used for training (e.g., SERE) US military personnel in resistance to interrogation.

In December, 2014, the Senate Select Committee on Intelligence issued a declassified 500 page summary of its still classified 6,700 page report on the Central Intelligence Agency (CIA) Detention and Interrogation Program. The report concluded that "the CIA's use of enhanced interrogation techniques (EIT) had presented no credible proof that information obtained through waterboarding or the other harsh methods that the CIA employed *prevented any attacks or saved any lives* (italics added). There was no evidence that information obtained from the detainees through EIT was not or could not have been obtained through conventional interrogation methods.

In June, 2015, in response to a critical assessment of China in the State Department's annual human rights report, China noted that the U.S., among other alleged human rights abuses, engaged in torture of terrorism suspects, specifically by waterboarding.

Writing in *The Nation*, April 25, 2016, in the article, "The CIA Waterboarded the Wrong Man 83 Times in 1 Month," with a subhead, "None of the allegations against Abu Zubaydeh turned out to be true. That didn't stop the CIA from torturing him for years." Rebecca Gordon stated:

- Donald Rumsfeld said he was "if not number two, very close to the number two person" in Al Qaeda.
- The Central Intelligence Agency informed assistant Attorney General Jay Bybee that he "served as Osama Bin Laden's senior lieutenant. In that capacity he managed a network of training camps … He also acted as al-Qaeda's coordinator of external contacts and foreign communications."

- CIA Director Michael Hayden would tell the press in 2008 that 25 percent of all the information his agency had gathered about A1 Qaeda from human sources "originated" with one other detainee and him.
- George W. Bush would use his case to justify the CIA's "enhanced interrogation program," claiming that "he had run a terrorist camp in Afghanistan where some of the 9/11 hijackers trained" and that "he helped smuggle al-Qadea leaders out of Afghanistan" so they would not be captured by U.S. forces.

None of that was true, according to Gordon.

He was Zayn al-Abidin Muhammen Husayn, better known by his Arabic nickname, Abu Zubaydah. And, when Rebecca Gordon wrote her article for *The Nation,* she believed he was still in solitary confinement in the U.S. prison in Guantanamo.

She writes:

Zubaydah was an early experiment in post 9/11 CIA practices and here's the remarkable thing (though it has yet to become part of the mainstream media accounts of his case): it was all a big lie. Zubaydah wasn't involved with A1 Qaeda; he was the ringleader of nothing; he never took part in planning for the 9/11 attacks. He was brutally mistreated, and in another kind of world, would be exhibit one in the war crimes trials of America's top leaders and its major intelligence agency.

Gordon writes that he was captured in Faisalabad, Pakistan and in the process was shot in the thigh, testicle and stomach. He might have died, she writes, if a U.S. surgeon flown in by the CIA, hadn't patched him up. Later, he lost his left eye "under mysterious circumstances," while in CIA custody.

The CIA hired two psychologists, Bruce Jessen and James Mitchell, to help interrogate Zubaydah. They were former instructors at the Air Force's SERE program (Survival, Evasion, Resistance, Escape). Their fee for helping the CIA: *$ 81 million* (italics added).

They waterboarded Zubaydah 83 times in one month; video-taped the interrogations and subsequently destroyed the tapes in 2005 when news of their existence became public. Subsequently a U.S. Senate report stated that Zubaydah would become "completely unresponsive" during those ordeals.

They also tortured Zubaydeh in 10 other ways, (which she describes) all approved by Jay Bybee, then serving at the Justice Department's Office of Legal Counsel.

Psychologists Jessen and Mitchell knowingly used Zubaydeh as a lengthy torture experiment, which not only violated International War Crime laws but also violated the U.S. War Crimes Act, which specifically prohibits experimenting on prisoners.

In September 2009, the U.S. government quietly withdrew its many allegations against Abu Zubaydah, Rebecca Gordon writes.

Gorden also said:

> The capture, torture and propaganda use of Abu Zubaydah is the perfect example of the U.S. government's unique combination of willful law-breaking, ass-covering memo-writing, and … "strategic incompetence." The fact that no one—not George Bush or Dick Cheney, not Jessen or Mitchell, nor multiple directors of the CIA—has been held accountable means that, unless we are very lucky, we will see more of the same in the future.

And Abu Zubaydah wasn't the worst case scenario:

Khakid Sheikh Mohammed was waterboarded *183 times* while being interrogated by the C.I.A.

8

Neologisms for Our Time

The neologisms George Orwell created for *1984* remain as unforgettable today as when Orwell conceived them 70-plus years ago: **Big Brother; thought police; thought crime; unpersons; double think; memory hole** and others—

There are now a whole set of new neologisms that would fit perfectly within the pages of Orwell's masterpiece:

- **Fake news:** Broadcast journalist Leslie Stahl related an off-camera incident with Donald Trump, about fake news, after he won the Republican nomination:

    "It's just me, my boss, and him—he has a huge office—and he's attacking the press. There were no cameras, there was nothing going on and I said, 'That is getting tired, why are you doing it?

    "You're doing it over and over and it's boring. It's time to end that, you've won the nomination. And why do you keep hammering at this?"

    "And he said: 'You know why I do it? I do it to discredit you all and demean you so when you write negative stories about me no one will believe you.'"

Fake news has become his favorite *meme* since his nomination. *(No other president has ever done this.)*

Some despots and authoritarian figures across the world have now adopted that term for use in their own countries, including Brazil under incoming President Jair Bolsonaro.

And, during the Republican National Convention, in Cleveland, in August 2016, Trump declared, "I alone can fix it," i.e., problems in Washington D.C.

That was pure Big Brother.

- **Alternative facts:** at the first news conference after Donald Trump's inauguration, Press Secretary Sean Spicer said "That was the biggest crowd to ever watch a presidential inauguration. Period." When reporters produced aerial photographs showing beyond a doubt that the first Barack Obama inauguration had far, far more spectators, Presidential aide Kellyanne Conway said Spicer was giving "alternative facts."
- **The Deep State:** A construct by Steve Bannon and his far-right cohorts or perhaps his far-far-right cohorts. The "Deep State" is purportedly an invisible government-within-the-government; members of the deep state must be discovered and dismissed. The fact that such an invisible government does not exist does not deter Bannon and others in believing it so.
- **Enemy of the People:** President Trump has repeatedly called the mainstream press the "enemy of the people." Critics and Trump biographers alike have stated that he has practically no attention span, has not read a complete book in his adult life and has little or no understanding of history.[6] The phrase "enemy of the people" was first

---

6 On October 30, 2018, President Trump announced he wanted to end "Birthright Citizenship," i.e.,. a person born in the United States becomes a citizen automatically. He claimed that the law offering citizenship to babies of non-citizens its "ridiculous" and "has to end." He claimed that he could end Birthright Citizenship with an "Executive Order." Birthright Citizenship is enshrined in the 14th Amendment to the Constitution; at the very least attempting to nullify this by an Executive Order would involve a lengthy legal battle, which the White House under President Trump may not have the legal team, or experience to undertake.

used in the Stalin years in the Soviet Union, meaning anti-Stalin forces.

In response to Trump's attacks on the press, the U.S. Senate passed a resolution August 16, 2018, affirming that the press is not "the enemy of the people."

The nonbonding resolution, which cleared the chamber by unanimous consent, also touted the "indispensable role of the free press" and said an attack on the media meant to "systematically undermine the credibility of the press (is) an attack on our democratic institutions."

And …

The Senate's action came hours after Trump launched his latest attack on the press, saying much of what is written is "fake news."

- **America First:** Like "Enemy of the People," Donald Trump seems to have no understanding of the origins of "America First." It was an anti-war committee formed to oppose America's entry into what became World War 11. Charles Lindbergh became its spokesman in late 1940. It was: anti-British; anti-Jewish and anti-Franklin D. Roosevelt. Lindbergh became reviled for his perceived anti-Jewish sentiments, which he denied. The America First committee disappeared when the Japanese attacked Pearl Harbor.
- **Truth isn't Truth:** On the NBC political commentary show "Meet the Press," Sunday August 19, 2018, Rudy Giuliani, former Mayor of New York City and then Donald Trump's lawyer-for-television made these statements with Chuck Todd, "Meet the Press" moderator:

  Giuliani: When you tell me that, you know (Trump) should testify (before Special Counsel Robert

Mueller) because he's going to tell the truth and he shouldn't worry, well that's so silly because it's somebody's version of the truth. Not the truth. He didn't have a, a conversation—

Chuck Todd: Truth is truth. I don't mean to go like—

Giuliani: No it isn't truth. Truth isn't truth.

Chuck Todd appeared dumbfounded by that lack of logic, gobsmacked, as the British say.

Writing in the website Maddowblog, the next day, August 20, Steve Benen said:

As outlandish as the claim was, the presidential attorney insisted he meant to say that. Indeed, Giuliani tried to defend it.

He specifically pointed to the dispute over Trump's alleged pressure on former FBI Director James Comey over the federal investigation into Michael Flynn, the disgraced former White House national security adviser. Giuliani and Trump say there was no conversation with Comey about Flynn, while Comey and his contemporaneous (notes) say the opposite. Therefore, according to Giuliani, there is no "truth."

But that's not what "truth" means. Trump and Comey may have competing claims about the same event, but that doesn't mean the truth doesn't exist; it means one of them is lying.

Nevertheless, what we're left with is the latest in a series of Orwellian attempts from Trump world to undermine empiricism. Giuliani, for example is on record saying, as part of his response to the Russian scandal, "I don't know how you separate fact and opinion." "Truth is relative." And just last week, <u>"Facts are in the eye of the beholder."</u> (Underlining is in the original text.)

And, Benen writes,

The president himself, meanwhile, continues to tell his followers that he should be considered the sole authority for truth. Trump told an audience last month, "Just remember: What you're seeing and what you're reading is not what's happening." A week later, the president added, "Polls are fake, just like everything else."

In 1984: The party told you to reject the evidence of your eyes and ears. It was their final, most essential command.

9

Beyond Orwell's Imagination …
Beyond Big Brother …

Washington, D.C.
February 19, 1942

Following the Japanese attack on Pearl Harbor, President Franklin Roosevelt signed Executive Order 9066 on that date, which allowed the incarceration of between 110,000-120,000 Japanese-Americans living on the west coast.

Sixty-two percent of those were American citizens.

It was thought, apparently, that if the Imperial forces of Japan invaded the west coast, all these Japanese-American citizens would rise up to sabotage the United States or otherwise help the invading Japanese.

There were 127,000 Japanese-American citizens living in the United States at the time of the Pearl Harbor attack; 80,000 were *Nisei* (second-generation American-born Japanese with U.S. citizenships) and *Sansei,* third-generation, the children of *Nisei.* The rest were *Issei,* immigrants born in Japan who did not guality for U.S. citizenship.

Later, it was determined that the decision to imprison all these Japanese-Americas was based on *race* rather than any security risk they might have posed for the United States.

Those with as little as 1/16 Japanese and infants with "one drop of Japanese blood" were sent to prison camps.

Roosevelt's Executive Order 9066 allowed the U.S. military to exclude all of those with Japanese ancestry from the west coast, including all of California and parts of Oregon, Washington and Arizona. The majority of the nearly 130,000 Japanese-Americans living in the United States were forcibly removed from their west coast homes in the spring of 1942.

5,000 Japanese-Americans were relocated outside the exclusion zones before March, 1942 and 5,500 community leaders were arrested immediately after Pearl Harbor and were in custody when Roosevelt's Order became effective.

The United States Census Bureau actively aided the military by providing confidential neighborhood census date on Japanese Americans. The Census Bureau denied this for decades, but finally admitted that in 2007.

Fred Korematsu sued the U.S government by appealing the Executive Order and his case went to the Supreme Court; the Court ruled against Korematsu. The Court ruled—narrowly— that the Executive Order was valid, but made no mention of the illegality of imprisoning U.S. citizens without just cause.

Nearly 40 years later—in 1980—President Jimmy Carter faced mounting pressure from the Japanese- American Citizens League and other civic groups; he appointed the Commission on Wartime Relocation and Internment of Citizens (CWRIC). The Commission issued a report, *Personal Justice Denied* and found little, if any, Japanese disloyalty and concluded the imprisonment *had* been the product of obvious racism and suggested that the government pay reparations.

In 1988, President Ronald Reagan signed into law the Civil Liberties Act of 1988, which apologized on behalf of the government for the massive imprisonment in the 1940s and agreed to individual payments of $20,000 (the equivalent of $41,000 in 2017).

The legislation admitted the government actions were based on "race prejudice, war hysteria and a failure of political leadership."

The U.S. government eventually paid more than 1.6 billion (the equivalent to $3,310,000,000 in 2017) in reparations to 82,219 Japanese-Americans who had been interned and to their heirs.

* * *

The internment of massive numbers of west coast Japanese-Americans in the 1940s was the **worst case of governmental prejudice, obvious inhumane mistreatment and "failure of political leadership" in the history of the United States ...**

UNTIL NOW.

News release
Department of Justice
Friday, April 6, 2018

Attorney General Jeff Sessions today notified all U.S. Attorney's Offices along the Southwest Border of a new "zero-tolerance policy" for offenses under 8 U.S.C. 1325 (a), which prohibits both attempted illegal entry and illegal entry into the United States by an alien. The implementation of the Attorney General's zero- tolerance policy comes as the Department of Homeland Security reported a 203 percent increase in illegal border crossings from March 2017 to March 2018 and a 37 percent increase from February 2018 to March 2018—the largest month-to-month increase since 2011.

"The situation at our Southwest Border is unacceptable. Congress has failed to pass effective legislation that serves the national interest—that closes dangerous loopholes and fully funds a wall along our southern border. As a result, a crisis has erupted at our Southwest Border that necessitates an escalated effort to prosecute those who choose to illegally cross our border," said Attorney General Jeff Sessions. "To those who wish to challenge the Trump Administration's commitment to public safety, national security and the rule of law, I warn you: illegally entering the country will not be rewarded, but will instead be met with the full prosecutorial powers of the Department of Justice. To the Department's prosecutors, I urge you: promoting and enforcing the rule of law is vital to protecting a nation, its borders and its citizens. You play a critical part in fulfilling these goals, and I thank you for your continued efforts in seeing to it that our laws—and as a result, our nation—are respected."

The Trump administration's "zero-tolerance policy" is this: to deter entry from Mexico and Central American countries, a couple entering the United States across the southwest border with a child, will be detained; the couple will be deported and the child would then specified as an "unaccompanied minor" and the child would remain in the United States.

Some children have been shunted off to New York City or elsewhere, without adequate records of who their parents were; where they were or where exactly the child was sent.

In the recent past, since this policy has been enacted, couples have signed documents—without an attorney present—indicating they left the United States voluntarily (and without their child or children). Some have signed documents—in English—that they could not read or comprehend.

This "zero-tolerance policy" quickly became a draconian nightmare of horrific proportions.

This is beyond George Orwell's imagination ... and beyond Big Brother's dystopic nightmare ...

Long-term consequences of this "zero-tolerance policy" were apparently never thought out by the Trump administration and there was no real "Plan B" to effectively return children to their parents.

Estimates now are that several hundred children may remain permanent orphans—as their parents were forcibly expelled from the border areas of United States, without any specifications of where their child, or children, were sent.

The late Philip Graham, publisher of *The Washington Post,* once described daily journalism as:

The first rough draft of history …

Sometimes misquoted as:

The first rough draft of a history that will never end …

His *daily-journalism-as-the-first-rough-draft-of-history* tells the continuing story of this debacle—these are just a fraction of the articles that can be found:

August 4, 2018

In this article, Angelina Chapin describes how children who left violence in Central America with their parents, presumably for a better life, will have to painfully remember their past:

KIDS WHO CAN'T TIE THEIR SHOES ARE BEING TRAUMATIZED IN IMMIGRATION COURT

Legal experts worry that children will be further traumatized by telling their horrific stories to judges and asylum officers.

by Angelina Chapin
The Huffington Post

She writes, in part:

In the coming months and years, many children who recently crossed the border will have to go through the traumatizing process of talking about their violent past in front of legal experts, judges and asylum officers. In the majority of cases, they will not have an attorney or parent by their side for support.

The U.S. immigration system was already daunting for migrant children before the Trump administration announced its zero tolerance policy on illegal entry into the country. Now, because more than 400 parents have been separated from their kids after crossing the border and deported, children who never expected to be on their own will have to navigate a complicated legal system without any parental support. (This week the government tried to dodge its responsibility to locate the hundreds of parents who were departed without their kids under the zero tolerance policy.)

Toddlers have already had to appear in immigration court without their parents. Legal experts worry about how children still not old enough to tie their shoes will be further traumatized by having to tell their horrific stores over and over again throughout the immigration process.

August 14, 2018

Government Agencies Coordinated to
Arrest Migrants Seeking Legal Status, ACLU Says

They timed interviews in such a way that would facilitate migrant arrests, according to a lawsuit filed by the ACLU.

by Willa Frej
The Huffington Post

Various branches of the federal government worked in tandem to time interviews with migrants in order to arrest and sometimes deport them more expeditiously, the American Civil Liberties Union of Massachusetts alleged in a lawsuit.

Emails made public Monday as part of the lawsuit that the ALCU filed against Department of Homeland Security Chief Kirstjen Nielsen show that U.S. Citizenship and Immigration Services communicated with Immigration and Customs Enforcement to schedule interviews with undocumented immigrants seeking legal status in such a way that would prevent the public from finding out about the arrests. The plaintiffs are immigrants who were handed orders of removal but are seeking legal status through their citizen spouses.

"These were coordinated arrests," Mathew Segal, one of the lawyers for the ACLU, told the Boston Globe. "And the marriage interviews that our clients had to go through were in fact set-ups."

There have been growing demands for the resignation of Kirstjen Nielsen, head of the Health and Human Services Department (HHS) but as of early November, 2018, she still serves in the Trump administration.

August 16, 2018

565 Migrant Children Remain Separated from Families 3 Weeks Past Judge's Deadline

The number of kids who have been reunited in the last couple weeks can be counted on two hands, according to court filings on the immigration detentions.

by Carla Herreria
The Huffington Post

Only small fraction of the nearly 600 migrant children reported to be still in the custody of the U.S. at the beginning of the month have been reunited with their families, according to a status update from the Trump administration filed Thursday.

In the court filings, lawyers for the U.S. Justice Department reported that a total of 565 children, including 24 who are younger than 5, remain in government-contracted shelters, separated from their parents.

More than two weeks earlier, the government had reported that there were 572 migrant children still in custody. That's seven more children than reported on Thursday, though lawyers noted that the total numbers on the reports are approximate as data continues to be updated.

In June, U.S. District Judge Dana Sabraw ordered the Trump administration to reunite the more than 2,500 children who were split up from their families as part of Attorney General Jeff Sessions' zero tolerance crackdown on illegal immigration.

August 23, 2018

I spent 5 Days at a Family Detention Center. I'm Still Haunted by What I Saw

by Catherine Powers
The Huffington Post

Powers traveled to the south Texas Family Residential Center in Dilley, Texas, to join a group of volunteers helping migrant women in detention file claims for asylum. She speaks Spanish and has a background in social work. Her article reads, in part:

> To be clear, this is a policy of deliberately tormenting women and children so that other women and children won't try to escape life-threatening conditions by coming to the United States for asylum. I joined this effort because I felt compelled to do *something* to respond to the humanitarian crisis created by unjust policies that serve no purpose other than to punish people for being poor and female—for having the audacity to be born in a "shit-hole country" and not stay there.

She also wrote:

> It was a nun who best summed up the experience as we entered the facility one morning. "What is happening here," she said, "makes me want to question the existence of God."
>
> I am still in awe of the resilience I witnessed. Many of the women I met had gone for more than two weeks without even knowing where their children were. Most had been raped, tormented, threatened or beaten (and in many cases, all of the above) in their countries (predominately Honduras and Guatemala). They came here

seeking refuge from unspeakable horrors, following the internationally recognized process for seeking asylum. For their "crime," they were incarcerated with hundreds of other woman and children in *la hielera* ("the freezer," cold concrete cells with no privacy where families sleep on the floor with nothing more than sheets of Mylar to cover them) or *la perrera* ("the dog kennel," where people live in chain link cages.) Their children were ripped from their arms, they were taunted, kicked, sprayed with water, fed frozen food and denied medical care. Yet the women I encountered were the lucky ones, because they had survived their first test of will in this country.

Some one recorded, presumably with a cellphone, the anguish wails of a young child, probably a toddler, inside one of these chain-link "dog kennels" …

> *momma … monma … momma … momma …*
> *momma … momma …*

Anyone who heard this replayed on major news networks (including the author of this book) could only describe it as beyond heartbreaking. (And the author of this book couldn't bear to hear it replayed) .

The recording was taken, or sent, to Washington, D.C., where it was re-played with loudspeakers outside the homes of Trump administration officials:

> *See—and hear—what you have caused—*
> *We don't do this in America—*

The national outrage was enormous.

September 17, 2018

The Trump Administration to Detain More Children and for Longer

The government plans to withdraw from a settlement that protects immigrant children from inhumane detention.

by Angelina Chapin
The Huffington Post

The Trump administration said Thursday that plans to withdraw from a court settlement that protects migrant children from being kept in detention centers under inhuman conditions and for more than 20 days.

If the government is successful, Immigration and Customs Enforcement will be able to run more family detention centers without obtaining state licenses, a requirement of the settlement, and more children will be kept in prison-like facilities for the duration of their immigration proceedings, which can last up to a year.

In June, the government said it was looking for space to house 12,000 more immigrants in family detention, and has now outlined new regulations that it claims preserve the "relevant and substantive terms" of the agreement. But experts say that ditching the 1997 Flores settlement, the result of a lawsuit surrounding the maltreatment of migrant children, will cause serious psychological and physical trauma for detained children.

"The government is saying, 'We don't really want to treat children humanely,'" said Bridget Cambria, an immigration lawyer who has represented detained families. "We want to subject them to the harshest rules we can."

September 19, 2018

Federal Agency Says It Lost Track of 1,488 Migrant Children

The Health and Human Services Departmentfirst disclosed that it had lost track of 1,475 children late last year, as it came under fire at a Senate hearing in April.

by Garance Burke
The Huffington Post

Twice in less than a year, the federal government has lost track of nearly 1,500 migrant children after placing them in the homes of sponsors across the country, federal officials have acknowledged.

The Health and Human Services Department recently told Senate staffers that case managers could not find 1,488 children after they made follow-up calls to check on their safety from April through June. That number represents about 13 percent of all unaccompanied children the administration moved out of shelters and foster homes during that time.

The agency first disclosed that its had lost track of 1,475 children late last year, as it came under fire at a Senate hearing in April. Lawmakers had asked HHS officials how they had strengthened child protection policies since it came to light the agency previously had rolled back safeguards meant to keep Central American children from ending up in the hands of human traffickers.

October 1, 2018

TRUMP ADMINISTRATION QUIETLY MOVES 1,600 MIGRANT CHILDREN TO TEXAS TENT CITY: REPORT

**The children have been relocated—
mostly in the middle of the night without warning—
from shelters and private foster care to
Tornillo in the Texas desert.**

by Dominique Mosbergen
The Huffington Post

More than 1,600 migrant children in U.S custody have been relocated in recent weeks from private foster homes ands shelters to a barren tent city in the Texas desert, *The New York Times* reported on Sunday.

Most of the children were moved "under the cover of darkness," and with almost no prior warning, according to the paper. They were roused from sleep in the middle of the night so they would be "less likely to try to run away," and loaded onto buses bound for the sprawling tent city in Tornillo, a border town in El Paso County.

The relocation is part of what the report called a mass reshuffling by the Trump administration, burdened by caring for 12,800 undocumented migrant children—a record number— now in federal custody.

October 2, 2018

New Trump Rules Keep Immigrant Kids Locked Up Longer. This Pregnant Mom is Terrified.

Six weeks after Iris Cruz was fingerprinted so that she could pick up her 14-year-old, she still hasn't seen her child.

by Elise Foley and Angelina Chapin
The Huffington Post

Thousands of undocumented children—even ones with parents or other adults eager to take them in—are languishing in U.S, government custody for increasingly long periods thanks to new background check and fingerprint screening requirements implemented by the Trump administration.

* * *

At least one mother is so desperate that she decided to sue.

Iris Cruz, who lives in Queens, New York, has been trying for months to reunite with her 14-year-old daughter, who was apprehended at the U.S. border in late July after fleeing Honduras. In early August, officials told Cruz that she'd have to wait a month to get fingerprinted. She managed to get it done sooner, on August 21, by going to the fingerprinting office to ask in person, and her partner provided his fingerprints soon after.

But six weeks later, she still hasn't heard anything about her daughter. So on Monday, Cruz sued the Department of Health and Human Services and its Office of Refugee Resettlement in federal court.

October 8, 2018

Migrant Children in Search of Justice: A 2-Year-Old's day in Immigration Court

by Vivian Yee and Miriam Jordan
The New York Times

The youngest child to come before the bench in federal immigrant courtroom No. 14 was so small she had be lifted into the chair. Even the judge in her black robes breathed a soft "aww" as her latest case perched on the brown leather.

Her feet stuck out from the seat in small gray sneakers, her legs too short to dangle. Her fists were stuffed under her knees. As soon as the caseworker who had sat her there turned to go, she let out a whimper that rose to a thin howl, her crumpled face a busting dam.

The girl, Fernanda Jaqueline Davila, was 2- years-old: brief life, long journey. The caseworker, a big-boned man from the shelter that'd been contracted to raise her since she was taken from her grandmother at the border last July, was the only person in the room she had met before that day.

"How old are you?" the judge asked after she motioned for the caseworker to return to Fernanda's side and tears had stopped. "Do you speak Spanish?"

And …

October 24, 2018

Agencies were surprised at Trump "zero tolerance" border policy, report finds

by Nathaniel Weixel
The Hill

Key government agencies were blindsided by the Trump administration's "zero tolerance" policy and had no plan in place to deal with the thousands of children who were separated from their parents, according to government investigators.

A Government Accountability Office report released Wednesday found that both the Department of Health and Human Services and the Department of Homeland Security were caught off guard when Attorney General Jeff Sessions released the "zero tolerance" memo in April.

Officials from DHS and HHS told investigators they were unaware of the memo before it was released, and did not take specific steps in advance of the memo to plan for the separation of parents and children of potential increases in the number of children who would be regerred to HHS's Office of Refugee Resettlement.

The "zero intolerance" policiy called for the criminal prosecution of all adult migrants who were detained after trying to cross the country's southern border. Any children brought across the border were separated from their parents, deemed to be "unaccompanied" and detailed by HHS in spearate facilities hundreds of miles from their parents.

But earlier, in her Twitter account, Homeland Security Secretary Kirstjen Nielsen wrote:

We do not have a policy of
separating families at the border. Period.
—June 17, 2018

Then, the ultimate denouement: by the end of 2018, two immigrant children died in U.S. custody near the southwestern border.

… end thoughts …

In the middle of the endless wars, the constant surveillance, the horrific "zero tolerance" debacle, with seemingly no end in sight, we are left with two thoughts; the first by Walt Kelly in the now long-gone- but-not-forgotten comic strip *Pogo:*

WE HAVE MET THE ENEMY AND HE IS US.

And the second thought is, now available on the internet, t-shirts inscribed thus:

MAKE ORWELL
FICTION AGAIN

George Orwell Bibliography

Down and Out in Paris and London. London: Victor Gollancz, 1933.

Burmese Days. New York: Harper & Bros., 1934.

A *Clergyman's Daughter.* London: Victor Gollancz, 1935.

Keep the Aspidistra Flying. London: Victor Gollancz, 1936.

The Road to Wigan Pier. London: Victor Gollancz, 1937.

Homage to Catalonia. London: Seeker and Warburg, 1938.

Coming Up for Air. London: Victor Gollancz, 1939.

Animal Farm. London: Seeker and Warburg, 1945.

Nineteen Eighty-Four. London: Seeker and Warburg, 1949.

Note: there have been a wide variety of Orwell anthologies and collections published posthumously, including a 20-volume collection, *The Complete Works of George Orwell,* edited by Peter Davidson. The first nine volumes are Orwell's fiction and non-fiction; volumes 10-20 include all of Orwell's known essays, poems, letters, journalism, broadcast reports and diaries, letters to his wife Eileen and family members. Included are many of Orwell's letters in newspapers and magazines and readers' reaction to Orwell's articles and reviews.

A very substantial (and highly-valued), 10-inch wide by 14-inch, 380 page, *Nineteen-Eighty Four: The Facsimile* edition was published by Seeker and Warburg in 1984. The facsimile edition reproduces the pages of Orwell's masterpiece in full-page size as they were originally hand-written.

Supplemental Bibliography

Bowker, Gordon. *Inside George Orwell: a Biography.* New York: Palgrave Macmillan, 2003.

Crick, Bernard. *George Orwell: A Life.* Boston: Atlantic, Little Brown, 1980.

De Tocqueville, Alexis. *Democracy in America.* New York: Signet, 2001.

Fensch, Thomas. *Behind* Islands in the Stream; *Hemingway, Cuba, the FBI and the crook factory.* New York: iUniverse, 2009.

_____. *Essential Elements of Steinbeck.* N. Chesterfield Va.: New Century Books, 2009, 2018.

_____. *The FBI Files on John Steinbeck.* N. Chesterfield, Va.: New Century Books, 2002.

_____. *Timeless (Pen) Names: The Life and Work of Charles Lutwidge Dodgson, Samuel Langhorne Clemens, Eric Blair and Theodor Geisel.* N. Chesterfield, Va.: New Century Books, 2018.

Hitchens, Christopher. *Why Orwell Matters.* New York: Basic Books, 2002.

Hotchner. A.E. *Papa Hemingway: A Personal Memoir.* New York: Random House, 1955.

Howe, Irving. *Orwell's* Nineteen Eighty-Four; *Text, Sources, Criticism.* New York: Harcourt, Brace and World, 1963.

Huxley, Aldous. *Brave New World and Brave New World Revisited.* New York: Harper Perennial, 1965.

Lewis, Peter. *George Orwell: The Road to 1984*. New York: Harcourt, Brace, Jovanovich, 1981.

Lewis, Sinclair. *It Can't Happen Here*. New York: Signet Books, 1970.

Meyers, Jeffrey. *Orwell: Wintry Conscience of a Generation*. New York: W.W. Norton, 2000.

Mitgang, Herbert. *Dangerous Dossiers*. New York, Donald I. Fine, 1988.

Ricks, Thomas E., *Churchill and Orwell: The Fight for Freedom*. New York: Penguin Press, 2017.

Shelden, Michael. *Orwell: The Authorized Biography*. London: Minerva Books, 1992.

Snyder. Timothy. *On Tyranny: Twenty Lessons from the Twentieth Century*. New York: Tim Duggan Books, 2017.

Steinhoff, William. *George Orwell and the Origins of 1984*. Ann Arbor: The Univ. Of Michigan Press, 1975.

West, W.J. *The Larger Evils: Nineteen Eighty- Four/ The Truth Behind the Satire*. Edinburgh, Eng.: Canongate Press, 1992.

Zamyatin, Yevgeny. *We*. New York: Penguin Books, 1993.

Notes

1   «Alexis De Tocqueville arrived … » Introduction,
     Democracy in America, Signet paperback ed., 2010,
     pp. 1.

1   "Born in Paris …" *Ibid.*, pp. 4.

2   "… was a classic liberal …" Alexis de Tocqueville
     Wikipedia entry.

3   *Chapter listings, Democracy in America,* Signet
     paperback ed., 2010, pp. v-viii.

6   U.S.-Russian superpowers, Tocqueville, Wikipedia
     entry. .

7   "In post-9/11 …" Gregorian, *Democracy in America,*
     2010 Signet paperback ed. pp. 375

7   "But—to paraphrase Lincoln …" Gregorian, *Ibid.,* pp.
     381-382.

11   "In the spring of 1928 …" Wikipedia entry, *Down and
     Out in Paris and London.*

11   … so as not to offend his parents … , *Ibid.*

12   "It is altogether curious …" *Down and Out in Paris and
     London,* Penguin Books paperback ed., 2013, pp. 13.

13   "You discovered what it is like to be hungry …" *Ibid.*
     pp. 15.

13   "You discover the boredom …" *Ibid.* pp. 15.

13   "Life on six francs a day …" *Ibid.* pp. 15.

13   "Clothes are powerful things …" *Ibid.,* pp. 130.

14   "And there is another feeling …" *Ibid.* , pp 16-17.

14   Publishing history, *Down and Out in Paris and
     London,* Wikipedia entry.

15   Four most university famous pseudonyms: Lewis
      Carroll, Mark Twain, George Orwell and Dr. Seuss in
      Thomas Fensch, *Timeless (Pen) Names,* New Century
      Books, 2018.

15   "corruption and imperial bigotry ..." Penguin Classic
      edition, 2009, cited in the Wikipedia entry, *Burmese
      Days.*

15   Jeffrey Meyers ... in Wikipedia entry, *Burmese Days.*
      Orwell quoted in Wikipedia entry, *Burmese Days*

16   "the lone and lacking individual ..." Emma Larkin
      Introduction, Penguin Classic edition, 2009, cited in
      Wikipedia entry, *Burmese Days.*

16   "From Flory ..." Fyvel, "A Writer's Life," in Orwell's
      Nineteen Eighty-Four: Text, Sources, Criticism, pp. 244.

Ernest Hemingway's protagonist Thomas Hudson, in *Islands
in the Stream* (Scribner's, 1970), is Hemingway himself to the
nth degree; same physical appearance, same personality, same
wives, divorces, sons. It is the most perfect *roman a clef* in
literature. Thomas Fensch, *Behind Islands in the Stream* (New
Century Books, 2009), pp. 119.

17   Flory birthmark ... , *Burmese Days,* Harcourt Harvest
      paperback ed., pp. 16-17.

17   "black stinking swine," in Wikipedia entry, *Burmese
      Days.*

17   Publishing history, in Wikipedia entry, *Burmese Days.*

18   *Traitor to His Class: The Privileged Life and Radical
      Presidency of Franklin Delano Roosevelt,* title of
      extensive biography of Roosevelt by W.H. Brands,
      Doubleday/Random House, 2008.

18   "unfair in some ways …" quoted in Larkin,
      Introduction, Penguin Classic edition, 2009.

18   Burmese literary awards, in *Burmese Days,* Wikipedia
      entry.

19   Christopher Hitchens and references to James Joyce
      and *Ulysses,* in Wikipedia entry, *A Clergyman's
      Daughter.*

20   Victor McHugh review in Wikipedia entry, *A
      Clergyman's Daughter.*

20   "Oughtn't to have published it." Orwell in *In Front of
      Your Nose,* reprinted in Wikipedia entry, *A Clergyman's
      Daughter.*

20   "… bring in a few pounds for my heirs," in Peter
      Davidson, *A Clergyman's Daughter, A Note on the Text,*
      in Wikipedia entry, *A Clergyman's Daughter.*

21   "Horray for the middle class," in the Wikipedia entry,
      Keep the Aspidistra Flying.

21   "Under the stress … ," Wikipedia entry, *Keep the
      Aspidistra Flying.*

21   "Money again …" from *Keep the Aspidistra Flying*, in
      Wikipedia entry.

22   Meyers, Orwell, The *New Statesman* and Mailer in
      Wikipedia entry, *Keep the Aspidistra Flying.*

23   Peter Stansky and William Abrahams, *Orwell: The
      Transformation,* pp. 134, cited in the Wikipedia entry,
      The Road to Wigan Pier.

24   blue tattoos, *The Road to Wigan Pier,* Harcourt
      paperback ed., pp. 36.

24   Diet listing, *Ibid.,* pp. 94

25   "frightful …" *Ibid.* pp. 79.

25   Slag-heaps … , *Ibid.,* pp. 105.

26   John Steinbeck section: "The Journalistic Background
      of *The Grapes of Wrath*" in Thomas Fensch, *Essential
      Elements Of Steinbeck,* New Century Books, 2009,
      2018, p. 43-57.

33   *The Harvest Gypsies.* Charles Wollenberg, ed. Berkeley,
      Cal.: Heyday Books, 1988.

46   "full of good criticism ..." Ruth Dudley Edwards,
      Victor Gollancz, a Biography, pp. 246-247.

46   "When the Fascist forces ..." Lewis, *George Orwell: The
      Road to 1984,* pp. 55.

47   "Every line ..." *Ibid.,* pp. 54.

48   "Orwell did not know ..." *Orwell in Spain,* pp. 6.

48   "A deposition was presented ..." Orwell, *Facing
      Unpleasant Facts,* pp. xxix.

49   "In the Lenin Barracks ..." Orwell, *Homage to
      Catalonia,* Harvest paperback ed., pp. 1.

50   "... a German Mauser rifle ..." *Ibid.,* pp. 17.

50   "P.S.U.C ..." *Ibid.,* pp. 47.

50   "and lice ..." *Ibid.,* pp. 76.

50   "so-called hospital ..." *Ibid.,* pp. 77.

50   "It was at the corner of the parapet ..." *Ibid.* pp.
      185-186.

52   "There was always a touch ..." T. R. Fyvel, in Irving
      Howe, ed., *Orwell's Nineteen Eighty-Four; Text, Sources,
      Criticism,* pp. 246-247.

53   "He finished ..." Lewis, in *George Orwell: The Road to
      1984,* pp. 67.

54   "... I saw a little boy," Orwell, Preface to the Ukrainian
      edition, *Animal Farm.*

55   "I believe *Gulliver's Travels* ..." W.J. West, *The Larger
      Evils,* pp. 62.

John Steinbeck's favorite book as a youth was a juvenile version of *King Arthur and the Knights of the Round Table.* Steinbeck's novel *Tortilla Flat* (1935), is an exact re-telling o the King Arthur fable, set in 1930s California "Steinbeck, the Paisanos and Monterey Bay," in *Essential Elements of Steinbeck,* Thomas Fensch New Century Books, 2009. pp. 27-42.

55　　　Napoleon as Stalin, and Snowball as Trotsky, in John Rodden, ed., *Understanding Animal Farm,* pp. 5f.

56　　　"The revolt of the animals … ," Wikipedia entry, *Animal Farm.*

58　　　"It is a book … ," Paul Owen, "1984 thoughtcrime? Does it matter that George Orwell pinched the plot?" *The Guardian,* Sept. 24, 2018.

63　　　"His family owned an estate …" Robert McCrum, The Masterpiece that Killed George Orwell," *The Guardian,* July 8, 2015.

63　　　"… mountainous bare and infertile," Jura, Wikipedia entry.

64　　　"Jurrasic Period," Meyers: *Orwell: Wintry Conscience of a Generation, pp. 256.*

64　　　"A tall, cadaverous, sad-looking …" McCrum.

64　　　"Writing a book …" Orwell in McCrum.

65　　　"It was a desperate race …" McCrum.

65　　　"Among the most terrifying …" Warburg, cited in 'McCrum.

66　　　Trotsky biography, Trotsky Wikipedia entry.

68　　　Thought Police, Wikipedia entry.

68　　　Beria and Yezhov, Wikipedia entry, *Nineteen Eighty-Four.*

69   "We had to destroy the village in order to save it," Zafar
        Sobhan, *The Guardian*, Oct. 24, 2018.

70   "George Orwell and the origins of the term 'cold war'"
        in: blog.oxforddictionaries.com, "George Orwell's 1984
        is suddenly a Best Seller." *The New York Times,* Jan. 25,
        2017.

72   "When he was alive …" Ricks, *Churchill and Orwell,*
        pp. 246.

72   65 languages … Wikipedia entry, *Nineteen
        Eighty- Four.*

72   "A half million copies …" Peter Ross, "Saving Orwell,"
        The Boston Review, Oct. 6, 2017.

73   "It was a bright cold day …" *1984,* American edition,
        pp. 3.

73   "The Ministry of Truth …" *Ibid.,* pp. 5.

81   "Winston could not remember a time … *1984*, U.S. ed.,
        pp. 33.

81   Civil War deaths … "New Estimates Raise Civil War
        Death Toll," *The New York Times,* April 2, 2012.

82   History of U.S. wars: "List of wars involving the United
        States," Wikipedia entry.

111   Charpentier, "America has been at war …" website
        Freakonometrics.

111   Length of U.S. wars: "List of the lengths of the United
        States participation in wars," Wikipedia entry.

114   "Why can't we stop our wars?" *Pittsburgh Post-
        Gazette,* May 18, 2011, retrieved from the internet.

Dan Simpson has been a ranking ambassador since 1990. Mr. Simpson retired from the U.S. Foreign service in 2001, after 35 years of distinguished service, which included tenure as the vice president of the National Defense University in Washington, D.C., and assignments to countries in Africa, the Middle East and Europe, including as U.S. ambassador to the Central African Republic, ambassador and special envoy to Somalia and ambassador to the Democratic Republic of Congo.

Africa has been the center of his diplomatic attention for four decades, beginning with a teaching assignment to Eghosa Anglican Boys' School, Benin City, Nigeria, for two years following his graduation from Yale University with a B.A in 1961. Mr. Simpson has held ambassador rank since 1990, and was ambassador to the Democratic Republic of the Congo (ex-Zaire) from 1995-1998; ambassador to Somalia, 1994-1995 and ambassador to the Central African Republic from 1990-1992. Other significant assignments included deputy chief of mission/ acting ambassador to Lebanon, 1987 to 1989, director of Southern African Affairs, Dept, of State, Washington, 1980-1984 and deputy commandant for international affairs, U.S. Army War College, Carlisle, Pa., 1993-1994.

Prior to his retirement, Mr. Simpson served as director of the Mission to Bosnia and Herzegovina of the Organization for Security & Cooperation in Europe (OSCE), a 55-member organization responsible for conducting elections, human rights monitoring and implementation of the 1995 Dayton Peace Accords that ended the war there.

117   "In the post 9/11 era," Thomas E. Ricks, *Churchill and Orwell*, pp. 255.

117   "It is a warfare ..." Orwell, in Ricks, pp. 225.

119   "Behind Winston's back ..." *1984*, U.S. ed. pp. 4 .

119   "For decades ... , " Stanley and Steinhardt, "Bigger
        Monster, Weaker Chains," The American Civil
        Liberties Union report, Jan. 2003.

119   Concept of the telescreen, W. J. West, *The Larger Evils*,
        pp. 176.

120   "Mass surveillance in the United States ..." in the
        Wikipedia entry "Mass surveillance in the United
        States."

123   "Early in the century ... ," Mitgang, *Dangerous
        Dossiers*, Ballentine paperback ed., pp. 1.

123   "... during Hoover's reign ..." *Ibid.*, pp. 7-8.

125   "It is commonly considered ..." John Steinbeck,
        Wikipedia entry.

126   Thomas Fensch's *The FBI Files on John Steinbeck*
        contains the complete Steinbeck/FBI files. (New
        Century Books, 2002).

128   "Hemingway's judgment ..." in Mitgang, pp. 44.

128   Floridita bar episode, *Ibid.*, pp. 50.

128   "It's the worst hell ..." A.E. Hotchner, *Papa Hemingway*.
        New York: Random House, 1966. pp. 266.

129   "Depressive/persecutory," *Ibid.*, pp. 275.

129   Under sedation and suicide attempts, *Ibid.*, pp. 286,

130   ECT treatments, *Ibid.*, pp. 276.

130   "There are some things ..." Preface, Hotchner, *Papa
        Hemingway*, from Hemingway, *Death in the Afternoon*,
        1932.

131   John Lennon, and other FBI file pages, Wikipedia
        entry, "Mass surveillance in the United States."

131   Church committee summary and findings and U.S.
        intelligence activities, in Wikipedia entry "Mass
        surveillance in the United States.

134   "Mueller: FBI uses ..." BBC, June 19, 2013 cited in
       Wikipedia, "Mass surveillance in the United States."

136   Roe vs. Wade case history, in Wikipedia entry, "Roe v.
       Wade."

143   Positions of U.S. political parties, in Wikipedia entry,
       "Abortion in the United States."

145   Norma McCorvey quotation in "Roe v. Wade" entry,
       Wikipedia.

146   "Black sites," from the Wikipedia entry "Black site."
       Names of the 17 ships used as floating prisons, cited in
       the Wikipedia entry "Black site" section, "Mobile sites."

152   Julia de Beausobre, in William Steinhoff, *George Orwell
       and the Origins of 1984*, pp. 41-42.

154   "Waterboarding is an enhanced ..." in "Does
       waterboarding work?" by Julie Tate, *The Washington
       Post,* Jan. 25, 2017, retrieved from their website, and in
       "Waterboarding," Wikipedia entry.

155   Waterboarding history in Wikipedia entry,
       "Waterboarding."

160   "In August, 2002 and March 2003 ..." in Wikipedia
       entry, "Waterboarding."

161   "The CIA Waterboarded the Wrong Man 83 Times in
       1 month," Rebecca Gordon, *The Nation,* April 25, 2016.

163   Khalid Sheikh Mohammed, in Wikipedia entry,
       "Waterboarding."

164   Leslie Stahl-Donald Trump incident, Ian Schwartz,
       RealClear Politics website, May 23, 2018.

165   Birthright citizenship (footnote). "Trump Wants
       to Order End to Birthright Citizenship," Willa Frej,
       Huffington Post website, Oct. 31, 2018.

166 "Senate takes shot at Trump, passes resolution affirming 'press is not the enemy of the people,'" The Hill website, August 16, 2018.

166 "America First," Wikipedia entry.

166 "'Truth isn't truth': Trump World targets our understanding of reality," Steve Benen, Maddowblog website, Aug. 20, 1018.

168 "The Party told you to reject ..." *1984,* U.S. ed. pp. 81.

169 West coast World War Two Japanese—American incarcerations, Wikipedia entry, "Internment of Japanese Americans."

173 Philip Graham quotation: Philip Graham, Wikipedia entry.

185 Two children died in U.S. custody, Elizabeth Cohen, "After children die in U.S. custody, authorities turn to nation's pediatricians for guidance." CNN website, Dec. 29, 2018.

187 *Make Orwell Fiction Again* t-shirts available on Amazon.

About the Author

THOMAS FENSCH has published nonfiction books since 1970; a partial list is at the front of this book.

He has published five books on John Steinbeck; two on Theodor "Dr. Seuss" Geisel; two on James Thurber; one each on Ernest Hemingway and Oskar Schindler; the only full-length biography of John Howard Griffin, the author of *Black Like Me,* and other nonfiction titles.

He has a doctorate from Syracuse University and lives outside Richmond, Va.

CPSIA information can be obtained
at www.ICGtesting.com
Printed in the USA
BVHW011531100519

547677BV00007B/16/P